WAITING
TO LIVE
AGAIN

LIVING AGAIN

*This is the story of my sister's life challenges, with her
illness of diabetes, and how she learn to truly except life not
for what it brought her, but what it taught her thru her
relationship with God, and how she began to live again!*

Mildred Jean Watkins

WESTBOW
PRESS®
A DIVISION OF THOMAS NELSON
& ZONDERVAN

WestBow Press books may be ordered through booksellers or by contacting:

WestBow Press
A Division of Thomas Nelson & Zondervan
1663 Liberty Drive
Bloomington, IN 47403
www.westbowpress.com
844-714-3454

Interior Image Credit:
MILDRED JEAN WATKINS/WITH: VALERIE CHRISTINA GRAHAM

Scripture taken from the King James Version of the Bible.

ISBN: 978-1-6642-1192-6 (sc)
ISBN: 978-1-6642-1194-0 (hc)
ISBN: 978-1-6642-1193-3 (e)

Library of Congress Control Number: 2020921988

Print information available on the last page.

WestBow Press rev. date: 12/30/2020

WAITING TO LIVE AGAIN

HAPPINESS IS LIKE A BUTTERFLY,

IF YOU KEEP GRASPING

IT WILL EVADE FROM YOU, BUT IF YOU LOOK AWAY

AND STOP DWELLING ON IT SOON

IT WILL LAND UPON YOU

ALL THINGS DON'T HAPPEN OVERNIGHT,

'SOME THINGS REQUIRE PATIENCE"

AND THAT'S HOW I BEGAN TO LIVE AGAIN

And the Lord directs your hearts into the love of

God, and into the patient waiting for Christ.

2 Thessalonians 3:5

I Can Live Again

I've been thru some things you were there with me

I almost gave up, you helped me to see

You taught me to love, you taught me to pray

How soon life can be taken away

You taught me to trust

You taught me to give

You taught me patience

You taught me to live

You sent Christ to show us the way

Living life as it's given to the full everyday

My life, my purpose, are all in your hands

Thank God you showed me how

I can live again

AUTHOR: MILDRED JEAN WATKINS

A Letter from the Author

It has been a privilege, and great joy for me to write this book for Valerie Graham, it has been fulfilling to share in making a dream come too, not just because you're my sibling, but because it may help someone else who needs to hear of the experiences you went thru, and be a help to them in some way. I'm glad to have played a part in telling your story so it can be shared with the world. Whenever we take time to give a portion of ourselves as a testimony to others, "even just a little bit", no matter how small or large the story may be, and the experiences we have been thru as Christians or even if you're not a Christian at this time, it becomes widespread, everyone has a story to tell, and by sharing your story others can receive a piece of your living testimony to help them in what they may be going thru, and that's what this book is all about "sharing the gospel of Christ" the absolute truth to help build Gods kingdom so others may become inherited sharers in what God has in store for us all, if we will except his Son today he's waiting with loving, and open arms, he loves us so much more than we realize. So as we become Christians throughout the world we become a huge colony of believers living, sharing, and growing in the Gospel of Christ that's what it's truly all about. May God continue to keep you forever broaden your horizon, strengthen your testimony, uplift your standards in Christ, and be a blessing to others in this world thru the manifestation of his word, for there is a better world yet to come, He said in his word in 1 Corinthians 2:9 Eyes has not seen, nor ear heard, nor have entered into the heart of man the things God has prepared for those who love him. May God truly bless you in what he has in store for you next, may you always continue to fulfill the purpose that you were intended to do here on earth for the glory and honor of God's Kingdom. Never give up, but endure till the end. Stay forever in God's word for it is his word that will always stand, envelop, and keep us thru this life, till we meet on the other side which is that great place called Heaven! I love you forever my beloved one may God richly bless, and continue to keep you in his loving arms for you are one of his chosen anointed ones, and I am his vessel to aide in spreading his word thru your life's testimony I love you forever, and ever may God bless you Amen.

Sincerely Yours,

Author: Mildred Jean Watkins

WAITING TO LIVE AGAIN

CHRIST CAME THAT WE MAY
HAVE LIFE AND LIVE IT ABUNDANTLY
TO THE FULL

Preface

VALERIE GRAHAM'S STORY OF HER NEAR DYING EXPERIENCE, OF HOW GOD BROUGHT HER THRU ALL HER STRUGGLES DURING HER ILLNESS WITH DIABETES, AND HOW HE BEGAN TO TURN HER LIFE AROUND INTO NOT JUST EXISTING, BUT TO REALLY LIVE HER LIFE TO THE FULLEST, AND START BY TRULY LIVING AGAIN!

JESUS IS HEAVEN'S DOOR TO LIFE AND I'M

WAITING TO LIVE AGAIN!

CHRIST CAME THAT WE MAY HAVE LIFE
AND LIVE IT ABUNDANTLY TO THE FULLEST
THE LIFE & NEAR DYING EXPERIENCE OF

VALERIE C. GRAHAM

Author: MILDRED JEAN WATKINS

VALERIE GRAHAM'S

Dedication

I first of all dedicate this book to God in heaven for it is he who deserves all the honor, and praise after all is said and done " I give him the glory", thank you Lord for opening my eyes, and showing me the clear picture of what you have in store for us all "which is the promise of an everlasting life" and so that we may live this life which you have given us even while we are existing right here on earth to its full potential while we are yet here in this world, and so that we may live our life in a way that is pleasing unto you God so we may have life thereafter so when dying comes our way, we may live forever with you God, and your Son who came that "we may have a chance to the tree of life", and live again with you our God in Heaven. This is Gods promise if we except Christ, and be sincere and ask him to forgive us of our sins, and come into our hearts as our Lord and Savior.

I also dedicate this book to my former Pastor Sherman G. Allen who "inspired me to share my testimony" so that I may be a blessing to others, in sharing the gospel of Christ our Lord and Savior.

To Elder Paul whom was my encouragement when he prayed for me as he prophesied that my blessing was in my testimony and that I need to tell the world about it.

To Prophetess Janice Mixon who prophesied that God said regardless of my fears he would still be able to use me, and not be concerned so much about my condition, but to except the purpose he has for me thru ministry to help others in this life.

I also dedicate this book to my earthly parent who has gone on to be with the Lord the late Reverend William Henry Graham Sr. who instilled the word of God in me, had it not been for the word I would not be here today, for God knew me before I was formed in my mother's womb "he has a purpose for my life", and he has a purpose for each of us, we are not our own for "we are all bought with a price", which Christ paid the price on the cross when he gave his life for you, and me that purpose is to be used within our body and spirit to glorify God for his kingdom thru the word of God. John 5:24 says Verily, Verily I say unto you, he that hears my word, and believeth on him that send me, hath everlasting life, and shall not come into condemnation, but is passed from dying unto life. When you except Christ as your personal Savior that is God's promise to you, your reward will be eternal life forever which means always, just imagine having a life that you've never dreamed of. Christ has prepared us a place with no limits beyond our wildest measures" we could ever dream of having such a wonderful life" with our God in heaven. Can you imagine what an amazing life he has in store for those that love the Lord, and we will live with him forever, and ever!

A Special Dedication

FROM: THE AUTHOR

I often wondered why I had not finished this book soon as I thought I might have, now I know that sometimes our minds are like a hidden pavilion with many sheltered thoughts on display for our view only until that precise moment to expose any of those thoughts some of it may be love, hate, jealousy, malice, vindictiveness, greed, or forgiveness. Sharing this particular thought in mind I must say that nothing is more important as when the time of which a person has indeed exist in this life, and for that reason alone I extend a special dedication of this book to La Russell Cole my deceased in law. He had such a vivacious spirit in the life he lived. He never met a stranger, always showed love to all his family, friends, or strangers. He so cherished life, never stood stand offish he never saved his feelings of expressions of love for later he always showed his love right then and there to his family, strangers, and friends.

   La Russell was the perfect example of living life to its full potential, expressing his love for others in such a unique way even when he was in pain. We love you in our heart, and will always remember your kind, and loving spirit you had for mankind. May your soul rest in peace, and may God's loving arms surround you when he sees his son coming home. You will certainly be missed by your family, and friends who are left behind, but we know one thing, and that is that God knows best for there is no more suffering on this side anymore for you, so sleep now in Christ name. I would also like to dedicate this book to my loving and kind hearted sibling William Henry Graham Jr. he had such a zest for life, and loved God, and his family, so well, besides, his daughter Tina who was the light of his life. He never met a stranger. There are so many good things I could say about him, I know and realize we all have some faults, but none I can find in such a loving young man as he was, he loved his pastor, and church family as well at the Church of Philadelphia in his home town here in Fort Worth, Texas. You too will always have a special place in our hearts, and will truly be missed.

May you rest peacefully in the arms of Christ, and may you hear the words well done my good and faithful servant from our Lord, and Savior, we your family love you now and forevermore, until then when we see you again in that great place in the sky called Heaven.

From: The Author: Mildred Jean Watkins

Introduction

I remember in the movie Forrest Gump as he quoted the words of his mother Mrs. Gump, "Life is like a box of chocolates" you never know what you're going to get, which is a fact, because none of us really know what we are going to get in this life, so it's up to each and every one of us to try to make the best of this life that we possibly can. To me life is more like a gift from God its sweet as candy, and in exchange we're given a chance to give in advance back to God to make it sweet, this precious thing called life that he's given to us, and to make it count for his glory and honor by the choices that we make. This book is for the unsaved, as well as the saved, it is based upon the life and near dying experiences that Valerie Graham went through, her purpose in telling this story is to share with the world, in hope that it may help someone else that may be going thru similar experiences, so they will realize how easy it is to take some of the small things in life for granted, and if by possibility you may have been given a second chance as she was to live life to its full potential to enjoy what God has given you, whether it may be your health, well-being, senses, family, the limbs on your body, or life itself it's all a gift from God so what you've been blessed with in this life, I want to hopefully help in some way to perhaps expand the potential of those gifts in other's as Valerie Graham was given the same opportunity thru ministry, and to be an inspiration to all, and be the person that you are in the eyes of God. So others in the world will see, and want a taste of the sweet life that God's given all of us. So "let go" of the old you, and get ready to live again!

VALERIE GRAHAM'S
Acknowledgments

I would like to acknowledge William Henry Graham Sr. for without the lessons he has instilled in me I would not be the person I am today, I thank him for his strength, character, integrity, and wisdom that he shared with me, and all my family during his time here on earth I thank him for the love he had for his family members, and church family. I thank my mother Lois Ruth Graham for her prayers, and sincerity for without prayer I wouldn't be here, and that's because both my parents took time, and prayed for me, and all my siblings daily.

I would like to thank my previous Pastor Sherman G. Allen for the drive he gave me to tell my testimony. His encouraging words have helped me in so many good ways.

To Elder Paul for your prayers & prophetic word, I sincerely thank you.

To Prophet Janice Mixon who encouraged me not to look at the outside, but look on the inside of what God has in store for me, she encouraged me not to give up, and prophesied that when I would write notes on paper it was not going to look right or seem to make any sense to me, but that somehow, someway it will happen, and not to give up for God will make a way out of no way, so be patient, and remember that things may not happen when you want them to, but God is an on time God so be patient, wait on him, and watch God move when the time is right. I remember the Red Sea when the People of Israel thought there was no hope, and behold God got them across the sea from Pharaoh's army in just a knick of time, so remember, no matter what you are going thru in this life, just trust in God for he's got your back!

I want to acknowledge Jean had it not been for you letting God use you to put my short notes into writing, and creating the things I wanted to say but couldn't, and being my second eyes due to my illness with Diabetes so the world can see things in my perspective point of view this book would have not been written for the world to see, and perhaps help someone in this life, so that they too may live again as our God in Heaven intended for us to in a way that is pleasing unto him. Thank you for the sacrifices you made in putting some of your own dreams on hold, and using that time for me to tell my testimony to the world so that it may be a blessing to someone else in helping to build God's Kingdom.

To my confidant Jimmie Bennett, I thank you from the bottom

of my heart for being my personal advisor, had it not been for you I may not have went in the right direction to get this book to become a reality for the world to see.

To Alice Pugh I thank you for being my mentor for preparing me for what God was getting ready to do, had I not received your wise advice, I would have not been equipped for what God was about to reveal unto me for his purpose for my life.

To Anthony Graham, I want to thank you most of all for all of your love, and support that you have given me throughout the years, you are one of my siblings I could always rely on for support no matter what, and for that, I thank you from the bottom of my heart you have been a great inspiration to me.

And I saved the best for last, to God who I give the glory, the honor, and all the praise I thank you for all my blessings, and for you sending your precious Son who gave his life, so we may have life abundantly, and that the world may have a chance to the tree of life, and for loving me so very much unconditionally, being with me every step of the way thru my journey, and continuously opening my eyes to the right way that is pleasing unto you Lord so that I can share with the world, and I can be a living testimony so they too may become heirs in your Kingdom, and help others in winning souls to Christ, so in the end you will get all the glory, the honor, and say well done thy good and faithful servant. I thank you Lord for carrying me when I fell in my Christian walk, giving me strength when I was weak, and near dying so many times, you kept on loving me even when I didn't deserve it, and giving me a second chance at life teaching, and showing me how I can truly live again, if I hadn't gone thru these storms in life which I know I had to go thru, I don't know where I would be, but you kept me Lord, and you helped me get thru, so I just want to say thank you God amen.

Contents

This Book Teaches You to Wake Up and Smell the Coffee for it is Christ that is our Maxwell House, so let go of the old you, and enjoy the rich aroma, and fulfilling life that God has given each, and every one of us while we are still here on earth for it is Christ that is the cream and sugar in our daily cup of enjoying life to its full potential for we are destined to live the good life as the Word explains in John 10:10. I am come that they may have life, and that they may have it more abundantly. So let Christ, fill your cup today "take a sip of the good life", and like mocha, began to enjoy the rich aroma, choice grade, and the taste of the good life that God has prepared for you and me. Like the cup of coffee we drink, God will fill your cup with his word which is the truth, and the life, but it's up to you and I what we add to it, like choosing cream and sugar what will you choose life or the bitter cup of dying, I prefer the cup of life.

CHAPTER 1

Life and Dying Are in God's Hands

Lying there staring out the hospital window from my bed, I remember that, I felt as if I were locked inside this body of mine, screaming to come out, longing so desperately to be set free. It was as though I were a butterfly that had been closed inside for ages, and finally, a door had been opened so I could fly away to freedom, I use the butterfly as an example of the way I began to see my life as God began to show me some things about myself. The butterfly starts out as a worm, the caterpillar, which is looked upon as something that rarely attracts the eye of people. Once the metamorphosis begins to take place, it starts to form into something amazingly beautiful.

It becomes something beautiful, and pleasing in the sight of God, and it begins to attract the eyes of people, and they began to

1

see the beauty of the butterfly. This is how God began to mold me; how God started to change my character, my actions, and some other things about me. This is how he began to form me into what is pleasing unto him. I often wonder now if we will see such a beautiful creature in heaven in some of the most amazing colors we never imagined. I compare myself to the butterfly simply because it is only a mere pint of how much more pleasing I want to be in the eyes of God. It was only after I unconditionally submitted myself to him. You see sometimes we freely must totally give ourselves to God. We must say, "Here I am, Lord, use me. Mold me into what you would have me be, not my will, but yours, Lord. What I want or think is not important anymore. I want to be pleasing unto you, so here I am, Lord, without hesitation". This is how a change in me began to come about.

He began molding, training, and instructing me. You see, God knows that when we're done deciding what is best for ourselves, and we're ready to listen to him. Then he will make us over. He won't do it unless we are willing; God will not force us to do anything we don't want to do, Of course he does chasten those whom he loves, but we have to be willing vessels. We have to say, "Here am I, Lord, use me and, make me over." Now I know what is required of me based upon my past performances, and I know I have been appointed to tell the world how God can change each, and every one of us, just like the changes in the caterpillar, no matter what our past may look like, His son, Christ, died on the cross for all humankind. He took upon our sins, went to the grave on our behalf, unlocked the keys of the grave, and he got up and rose early one morning, so that we may live again, He paid the price; he can wipe our sins away, for Christ is that rock upon which we can build a clean foundation.

And like the butterfly, you can become something beautiful in the sight of God. As you emerge, and evolve from a sinner to a Christian through his power, you will shine in the eyes of people because everyone who knows you, or sees you will know there is a wonderful change in you. You will be changed, and flee away swiftly. The only difference, people, is that you will flee away from the dangers of sin, yet you can still enjoy life in a pleasing way to God. That's why he sent his precious son, Christ so that we may enjoy life while we're here on earth. God created earth, and put humans here to enjoy the things he created. He wants us to enjoy them by obeying the instructions he has given us in his Word. I'm sure most of you have heard the story of how God gave Adam and, Eve the Garden of Eden, and how he told them they could simply enjoy everything in that garden except the forbidden tree, which was the tree of good and evil. He warned them that they would surely die.

Eve ate of the forbidden fruit, and offered it to Adam, and he ate of it also. They failed to follow God's instructions, and that's what

3

got them both in trouble. So they became ashamed and tried to hide from God. The same thing applies to us; God wants us to enjoy this life he has given us, but he wants us to enjoy it in the right way a respectful way that is pleasing to him. I'm sure there are others in this world who may have felt the same as I once did, not having a clue that we as Christians can also enjoy life, and that God wants us to be happy. It is his will that we have an enjoyable life, in the right way, which is his way. If he wanted us to enjoy life our way, we would be in for a life of turmoil and sin, and dying. The Word says in Romans 6:23, "For the wages of sin is death, but the gift of God is eternal life which is through his son Christ, God's gift to us."

I just want you to know that you can still enjoy life as a Christian and not feel as if you are doing something wrong every time you turn around. Believe me when I say those days are over, and done with. Some of us may remember the fanatics as immaculate Christians you know the ones who act as if they have no sin. Remember in John 8:3-7 when the teachers of the law and the Pharisees brought in a woman caught in adultery? They made her stand before a group, and told Christ she was caught in adultery. The laws of Moses would have such a woman stoned. Christ bent down to the ground, and then he straightened up after they kept on questioning him. Christ replied to them, "If anyone of you is without sin let him be the first to throw a stone at her." And they all walked away one by one. Christ then asked her where everyone went. He asked if anyone condemned her. She said no one had. And Christ said, "Then neither do I condemn you replied, Christ "go now", and leave your life of sin."

Well that's the way Christian fanatics were, back then "always ready to judge". They perhaps believed if you even so much as breathed the wrong way you were doomed to go straight to the pit of the grave. God never intended for life as a Christian to be impossible. We can enjoy life, just not as the world does. We don't have to live in sin, but we can still live a good life, and feel free to enjoy life itself. We do not need to feel guilty as long as we are in the true will of God. That's why he has given us his Word in the bible, it gives us basic instructions. For everything we do in life there is an answer in his Word, that's why we must study his Word, and meditate upon it so God can give us an understanding of his Word. He helped me figure that one out through staying in his Word, and applying the Word of God to my life. Some of us don't realize what it truly means to live, and I don't mean just being alive, but truly live, and enjoying ourselves with this life that God has built for us.

He has laid the foundation; all we have to do is stand on it, and that foundation is his Word. It is the Word that will get us through this life, and it will be so much better than what we could have ever imagined if we'll only believe. I now know how precious every moment of life is, and how we should take it upon ourselves to cherish every moment of life, and how we should take it upon ourselves to cherish every moment that God gives us. It is so gratifying to him when we enjoy the good life he has chosen for us. We should treasure every moment that we have on this earth, and count our blessings. I remember in the scripture that says, John 10:10 "The thief cometh not, but to steal, kill, and destroy, but Jesus came that we may have life, and have it more abundantly." Just think about it, God loved us so much that he sent his only begotten son Jesus, here to earth, not only for the sins of humankind, but so that we may have a good life and be able to enjoy it to "the greatest decree". Now that is a loving God!

How awesome and loving can someone be to want us to enjoy life so tremendously, as I lay there in my bed strongly contemplating these thoughts in my mind, that was the day when I was in the Medical Building, and I had just recently had a near dying, experience in a comatose state not knowing if I was going to even survive, out of that transition of being unconscious for a while, but I held on to my faith in God, for life and dying is in his hands. Jean had been on her way to the Medical Building earlier in the week I heard, as the tears began running down her cheeks, praying to God, and saying I can't take it anymore she would make her way to the Medical Building often daily I heard, her worrying about me took a toll on her so heavily, especially after she heard from my other siblings that I may not make it through after the surgery. We had already lost our in law Juanita she, and Jean used to be very close at one time, and Jean's pastor had also passed away shortly after our in law Juanita passed, the late Reverend Gregory Spencer also known as the founder of Spencer's Funeral Home in Fort Worth, Texas, sometimes loss of loved ones in our lives can often take a toll on a person. One evening as she was driving to the Medical Building she had just got off from work that day, and in the midst of her driving she saw a white dove that flew by right before her eyes, it was as if God were giving her a sign, she began to fill a comfort in knowing that everything would be alright. Sometimes we just have to let go, and let God, and trust in him for life and dying are in his hands, he knows what's best, and will handle all of our troubles, so when we'll put our trust exclusively in him, and not in man he'll turn things around in our favor, and God will show up, and show out every time, for he will handle our storm, he's just trying to let us know I got this, if you'll just let me handle it all by myself, God is in control of every condition no matter what because you see he needs no help in handling our situation, sometimes we try to handle things on our own, and every time we fail simply because we're looking at our circumstance, but if we focus on God, and depend on him to get us thru our storms in life he won't fail us, so don't worry about what your situation looks like, he's saying I'm God Almighty, the same God that appeared back in the day unto Abraham, Isaac, and Jacob by the name of God Almighty in Exodus 6:3. He's the same God today that he was on yesterday, what he did back then for them he'll do the same for you God will have no respect of person if you'll just trust him you'll be alright because there is nothing or any situation that God can't handle. The people of Israel as I remember their circumstance looked very slim when they were being followed by Pharaohs army, but when Moses obeyed God, and stretched out his rod, the Word says in the book of Exodus 14:22 and the people of Israel went unto the midst of the sea upon the dry ground, and the waters were a wall unto them on their right hand, and on their left, so God showed up, and showed out and made a pathway thru the red sea, but look at this when the Egyptians pursued to follow them in the sea, God sent down a pillar of fire, and cloud at the Egyptian army, and threw it into confusion, he made the wheels of their chariots come off so that they had difficulty driving, sometimes the enemy will think oh I got you now, but God will make it hard for the enemy to harm us, he said in his word Isaiah 54:17 No weapon formed against you shall prosper, so see if we'll just trust him, God's got our back, he'll make things hard for the enemy to harm us, if we'll just wait on him. So what the enemy meant for bad, God will turn that thing around for our good, so he's got the upper hand on the enemy; all power is in God's hand. So when the people of Israel saw the power of the Lord displayed against the Egyptians, in Exodus14:31 the Word says the people feared the Lord and put their trust in God, and in Moses his servant, sometimes we have to take a leap of faith, now if the Israelites had been fearful to walk thru those walls of water, they wouldn't have made it, but when they saw God's power they began to trust him, and that's all we have to do today is just say God I'll trust you, my life is in your hands, so I'll trust you Lord because I know that you've got my back, no weapon formed against me shall prosper because he'll be with you every step of the way, and because of Moses obedience to God the people of Israel they made it thru to the other side.

1 Samuel 15:22 says behold, to obey is better than sacrifice. So when we are obedient to God, and don't sell out for something less, but stand still on his word, then we will see what he has in store for us is of much greater value if we'll be obedient, and stand on his word. As I began to look back over my past how sometimes I felt as though I had to struggle for my life, different ones trying to tell me how to live my life especially my parent, telling me you need to do this or you need to do that, don't get me wrong there's nothing wrong with your parent giving you advice, but when you're an adult, parents must allow you to make your own decisions, some of it was good advice, but at times I felt as if the walls were just closing in on me, and I just wanted to scream help me Lord!

Have you ever felt as if the walls are just closing in on you? So now you began to feel as if you don't know if you should go in one direction, or if you should go in the other direction, and I felt as if I had to satisfy everyone but myself, I remember telling my parent once that I wanted to go places, and do things, and "she ask me why", I said momma you've had a life, you've been married, had sons, and daughters, I haven't ever even had a male companion, I felt that she, and other females in my family were the only ones who had a chance to have somewhat of a life other than myself, even as I entered into these phases in my life, I had been battling with some issues within myself to help me not to give up on life, but to know that God is carrying my every burden, and he won't allow no more on me than I can bare, he promised me this in his word, but when I stopped to think about my life I began to dwell on the positive things, and not my circumstances, I stopped having that pity party with myself, and he began to show me that I don't need a man to make me happy of course God wants us to be happy in life, and he also wants us to have a mate in life if that is our hearts desire but, God showed me there's a difference in being alone, and being lonely, and when you've got Christ you are never alone because he's right there no matter where you are even to the ends of the earth he's still there he will never leave you, nor forsake you even when other people in life will disappoint you, Christ will never forsake us we may leave him, but he'll never leave us, he's always there waiting for us to make the right move because he loves us so much. So the key to happiness is first to love God, and then you must learn to love yourself not in a boastful kind of way, but you must care enough about your own self to not let someone else bring negativity into your life, if that person is going to cause you the opposite of happiness then you don't need to bring that person into your life, and settle for less, I'm not saying that everyone will bring you negativity, but you have to at some point learn to trust, and know who to trust, and when you receive the Holy Spirit it will lead and guide you, as you listen for the whisper of God's voice he will let you know in some way if this person is right for you or not, even in just friendship relations God will lead us & direct us in the right path of who is for you or against you.

There are some people that will bring happiness and joy into your life for maybe just a season, but you must wait on God, and seek him first. Matthew 6:33 says but seek ye first the kingdom of God, and his righteousness and all these things will be added unto you. God will send you the right mate if you seek him first, and this is your desire of course everyone is not meant to be married, and if so when you've got Christ you've got joy within, and nothing can take that away no man, no woman, not even the world, because Christ lives inside of you, and you'll be so much at harmony with yourself, however if your desire is to have a mate and you'll trust and be pleasing unto God first, then anything you desire he will give unto you, that's a promise in his word. Psalms 37: 4 delight thyself also in the Lord and he shall give thee the desires of thy heart.

I began to think on how God was beginning to heal me in so many other areas, not only in relationships, but in so many other areas of my Life and, yes I lost my leg, but even after losing a limb, there's healing afterwards, so I didn't dwell on the negative things in my life, but I began to think of his goodness, and how I could have been deceased there in that medical bed and how God spared me because it wasn't my time yet for he has a purpose and plan for my life, and in exchange for his gift of life, I will forever praise him, making every day count fulfilling my purpose here on earth, and use it to glorify his name. There are many people who have experienced dying, and came back because it was not their time to go yet, so God allowed them to come back to finish what he wanted them to do here on earth. I truly believe that no one who has ever experienced dying were given a second chance at all just for themselves, none of us were put here on this earth for our own benefit, but we are here to be a help to one another, and we should have joy in doing so.

I often listen to the hymn "Smile" by Kirk Franklin, some of us Christians we don't smile enough, we should set examples for the unsaved showing the world how great it is in living our lives for Christ, and wanting to let the world know, and to show how happy we are that he came into our life, and to tell them how much it will be a joy to have Christ in their lives as well, the world is looking for something different, there are hurting people out in the world who need to know that Christ loves them, and cares for them they need peace in their lives they are looking for an answer, and it is up to us as Christians to give them that answer which is Christ. Christ will bring joy, and peace in their lives, and we are his hands to let the world know, and we as Christians should want the world to share in having the joy that we have on the inside people are suffering in their homes, and around the world we must show them through Christ who lives in us that we love them in everything that we endeavor to do, God sees all, and he knows all.

The power of life and dying are in his hands, God is in control I once heard someone say, no God is not in control, he gave man dominion over the earth, but oh yes he is in control, he's only gave man so much power over the earth, but if man decides to disobey, and not do as his word has instructed man as Adam did, then man will be punished accordingly, he has the whole wide world in his hands as the hymn goes. In his word he said Deuteronomy 30:19 I have set before you, life, and dying, blessings, and evil, now choose life, so that you and your family may live, so we all must be about God's business and do what is necessary so that we too can help others, some people may say I have my own problems, but if we will stop looking at ourselves, and look unto God he will give us double

13

for our trouble, I'm reminded of the character Job in the Word, Job 1:6-12, and how when God allowed Satan to harm Job for he was one of God's chosen servants, a perfect and upright man who despised evil, and how God told Satan he could mess with everything except his soul, and Satan began to bring harm to Jobs body with many sores on his skin, and that would not turn him away from the love of God, so he assaulted him thru his cattle, his friends, family, and then his woman even told him why don't you blaspheme God and just die, but yet Job didn't listen to his woman, and he held on to

God's unchanging hand, in turn Job received double for his trouble he was blessed twice as much as with what he had before sometimes we can listen to the enemy which is Satan, and miss out on our blessing if Job would have listened to his woman, and what she had to say or his family, and his so call friends he would have missed out on what God had in store for him, but instead he held on with everything in him. So as I looked at Job, and all he went thru, I saw myself like Job, and I wasn't going to give up on God because he didn't give up on me sometimes we cease to realize how precious life really is, we allow all of our circumstances to really overtake us, and the whole time God is saying he has our life in his hands no matter what comes our way he knows all about us, God knows what we are going to do, and not do even before we do it, there are times we are put thru a test, sometimes a test is necessary this lets you know how strong you are, and what you've learned, when we were a child in school we always had to have a test this would let the teacher know if you were ready to go to the next level and beyond or not, this is the same way it is with God we have to go thru in order to get to the next level, the only good thing with God is he gives us a second chance to get it right. So when we're going thru our struggles in life just remember trials and tribulations don't last always, that morning will soon come after a while, and everything will be alright if you'll just hold on to Gods unchanging hand as Job did. Remember John 10:10 the enemy comes as a thief, to slay, and destroy, but Christ came so we would have that abundant overflowing life. One of the things that I have experienced in my life was the fear of dying, which fear is nothing but "false evidence appearing real", and God helped me to come to grips with this, and to know that he has every part of my being in control he told me that I shall live and not die, that's his promise to us when we keep his commandments, not to say that we will never die on this earth because it is appointed to every man to die soon or later, but there is life after dying if we choose the right way in this life so stay in his word, and be obedient to his word, trust God with our life in the midst of it all.

He has reminded us in his word, Acts 17:28 for in him we live, move, and have our being. For we are God's sons, and daughters my life, and yours are in his hands, I encourage everyone not to take life lightly, and I now look at life as a great opportunity to give back to God for all that he has done, for me in my life for he is so worthy his son Christ took all of our sins upon him, he knew what he was about to face, and told God not my will, but thou will be done, he was crushed for all of our transgression, went to the grave in our behalf, and rose again. How can we not love, and except him for all he did on our behalf none of us would have took the suffering that Christ did for us on the cross, and he did it simply because he loved us, he asked God when they were crucifying him to forgive them for they know not what they do. Even then he loved us enough to not hold us responsible for what was about to happen, and we can show him how grateful we are by giving back to God when we love one another, and when we show that love by our actions in how we treat one another daily, even by what we say to one another. In the book of Proverbs18:21 the Word says dying and life are in the power of the mouth.

We must be careful what comes out of our mouth for out of the overflow in the heart the mouth speaks is what he said in his word in Matthew 12:33, and in verse 12:36 he speaks that every man will give in account of every careless word they have spoken on judgment day. So be very careful of the words you say to others, sometimes it may be too late to take it back or apologize, life is not promised to any of us tomorrow. There will be ups and downs in our future, we all will experience our own challenges in life, don't give up your inheritance rights to be with God, unlike Esau he failed to make an effort to do what is right, and did what was easy, but there are always some consequences behind choosing what we think is the easy way out which is our way, and not Gods way, and if you're not sure about what to do go to the word of God, for there is an answer to every problem we may have in life, you can go to Gods word. There is life in the word, Proverbs 12:28 says in the way of righteousness is life and in the pathway thereof there is no dying.

Remember that life and dying are in God's hands. As I lye here in my bed I began to think of the goodness of God, and how he allowed me to come back, not every man or woman will have that favor on their life, but he allowed me to come back and let the world know that Christ lives, and he will live in you & me if we will let him, he gives us free will God is a powerful God, but it has to be our choice to choose life or dying, not saying that he won't pursue to chasing us sometimes God will do everything he can to save us because of his love for us, but it has to be our choice. He's got all power in his hands, he rose on the third day according to the scripture in 1st Corinthians 15:4, he got up with all power, in 1 Corinthians 15:55 he said O dying where is thy sting? Oh grave where is thy victory? The Word says in Ecclesiastes 8:8 there is no man that hath power over the spirit to retain the spirit, neither hath he power in the day of dying. So only God has the power to control life and dying if it's time for you to go, when dying comes your way then you're gone, so it pays to be ready when your time is up here in this life, because there is another life after this one, and that's eternal life, where you choose to live eternally will be your choice whether it may be Heaven or the grave.

A nonbeliever would perhaps say, well how do you know that? I know it because God said it in his word, and that person may say well I don't believe in God, and the word says in Psalm 14:1 The fool hath said in his heart, there is no God, Webster Dictionary defines a fool as one that is a swindled of a trick, "which is a trick of the devil", and it goes a little further to define a fool as one who is deceived, and deceive defines to make a person believe what is not false, and who do you think that is? Satan, then it goes a little further as to define deceive as mislead which is to lead in the wrong direction, to lead into wrong doing, and who do you think that is? Again Satan, so if you're going to believe what is correct then that makes you to be wise, in making a good decision, and not a fool and make a foolish decision, and allow yourself to be tricked by Satan, and don't let Satan lead you to deception believing things that aren't correct the choice is yours, and mine where we will spend eternity in Heaven or the grave because everyone won't get the chance that I did for God to allow you another chance to get it right.

For the Lord gives and the Lord takes blessed be the name of the Lord. I remember one night when I was over to my godparent's house, I found myself one night in such a deep depression which is nothing but an evil spirit, I was so depressed that I began walking alone, alongside the bridge that night, there were no cars coming by so I took my left leg, the very same leg that I lost during my surgery, I can remember I was ready to jump, and take my life, and I heard this still voice say to me, why would you take something that you didn't give, I didn't realize it then, but now that I think about it God was telling me then that he holds the power of life, and dying and it wasn't mine to decide to end my life. I found myself going back to the house and going into a part of the house which was a washroom, and falling down on my knees crying out to God, and asking him to please help me I needed peace of mind, have you ever needed peace before? It will drive you crazy sometimes if you don't get some peace, I remember back in the day when we were just a child, and sometimes our parents would say, you kids are getting on my last nerve, I need some peace, is there anyone out there that needs some peace today?

God will give you that peace of mind. My godparent came in that night and told me that I had a telephone call, it was one of the elder women at my church, she told me Val talk to me I can help she said, she was telling me to pray, I really couldn't pray at the time so I just began crying out help me Lord, please Lord help me right now, and then her words were Val, I need for you to start singing this hymn, "I am free, praise the Lord I'm free no longer bound". I began to repeat those words, over, and over until I felt those words deep in my heart there was a heaviness that began to lift my spirit. So when I went to church early that Sunday morning, the praise soloist confirmed the same hymn that day, and so even as I went to church that morning I had made up in my mind that I would not be singing on the praise team anymore nor would I be singing in the choir, so I found myself sitting in behind where the elder women of the church were seated.

When the pastor began to minister he said "the thing that the devil is trying to destroy you with, that's the thing he's going to destroy before it destroys you", so that sermon stuck with me, God has given me this second chance in life, and ever since then I can say I'm still here because I know that my life was in God's hands. He was there all the time to help me get thru every trying time that I ever experienced, God was there, and he carried me when I became weak, and could not seem to get thru a difficult situation by myself, God was there saying just trust me, and I will get you thru this for you are going to make it, I have more work for you to do yet. So I'm a living witness to tell the world that no matter what you may be going thru, God is there he knows your every pain, he knows your sorrows, and he is there for you, so just trust him, he will help you thru it all because he loves you, you are his, and he cares for you, your life is in his hands, Satan can't take your life, he doesn't have the power to, if God says it's not your time yet, all power is in his hands, my life, and your life are in the hands of God, and no devil in the grave can take that away from you. God, he's got all the power, not man, not Satan, but God's got all the power in his hands alone. As I think back over my life I can remember so many times when the enemy "Satan" tried to take me out, but God said not so, I was in church one time, and my dad was praying for someone in the church that day, my dad kept telling me Val wake up, and he ask the church to pray, and for no one to fall asleep, one of my siblings told me later that my parent said he saw this demon jump inside of me as I was sleep, he came over immediately as my eyes began to roll in my head, which I believe was a spirit of illness, and my parent ask the church to begin to pray, it was Satan who tried to take me out back then, but God had control of the situation even then.

I remember when I was coming home from work one day, when I was very young, and I was confronted by dogs every block I passed about two to three dogs began to start following me, and I remember Jean had always told me to not act as if I was frightened when I come upon a dog because they can sense your fear. So as I continued walking I looked back, and there was approximately around twenty

21

dogs following me so I kept on walking, one car passed by, and a man driving asked me are those all your dogs, and I said no, "I don't know who they belong to" they just started following me. The man kept on driving down the street, and so the closer that I got home the dogs stop following me about two or three at a time the last block I came to there was only one dog behind me, and he followed me all the way home to the back door, so when I went to open the door he looked up at me as if he wanted to come in, and I told him no I can't let you come in because you belong to someone else. The dog looked up at me pitifully as if he wanted me to be his master, and I told him again no I can't let you in you have to go now so he finally went away as I began to think, it seemed as if those dogs were my angels, and they had an assignment to make sure that I got home safe and sound, anything could have happen to me on the way home, the man who stopped in the car could have abducted me or anything could have happen, but with those dogs following me no one was going to bother me with that many dogs following.

So no weapon formed against me could prosper because those dogs had an assignment, and that was to cover me till I made it safely home, again God was in control. I remember another situation I was confronted with one day I was at home by myself cleaning the house, and some of us in this world have the gift of being able to see spirits, or demons, so I remember looking to clean under my bed, and so I reached my hand under the bed, and as I looked I saw this demon in the figure of a man with half of a body, and he went to reach for me, and said I'm going to get you, and I knew right then it was a demon, so I immediately said no you're not, that's one thing as Christians when the enemy comes our way we have to boldly speak to the enemy, and put the word on him I said no weapon formed against me shall prosper, and Satan you've got to go. So I remember my pastor had told us to drive evil spirits away to get some ammonia, so I went and got some ammonia cleaned the windows in the room, and from that day on I never saw that demon anymore, so you have to speak it, and believe it, once again God was in control.

I also remember the time when my dad, and his in law Earl were in the company van that of whom my parent worked for, and they were in an accident on the road, the van flipped over it was said about three times, and neither my parent, nor his in law came out of the van with not one scratch or bruise on them, God is in control all the time. I could go on with testimony after testimony, it just lets us know that all power is in Gods hand, and he is the one to say when it's our time to go, no matter what the physician says, what looks very slim of a situation God can bring us out just like in the Word the three Hebrew boys Shadrach, Meshach, and Abednego who failed to bow down to worship the image of gold set up by Nebuchadnezzar, and when they were put in the fire fiery furnace all of them came out without a burn, or scorched clothing nor a smell of smoke on none of them.

The king thought he could take them out, but all power was in the hand of God as the story is told in the book of Daniel, Daniel 3:14 the word states the king Nebuchadnezzar was astonished, and rose up and said to his counselors; did we not cast three men in the fire? They answered and said correct Oh king, he then answered lo I see four men loose, "walking in the midst of the fire, and "they have no hurt, and the form of the fourth is like the son of God so once again God was in the midst of it all, so just remember life and dying is in the hands of an almighty God that I serve, he's on high, and he sees low so can't nobody take us out until God says so, but be ready when he comes so we must make a decision to except him today for tomorrow is not promised, tomorrow may very well be too late. We have a chance to get it right while the red fluid is flowing warm in our veins. Christ is the answer for the world today he's waiting patiently on you with his arms stretched out wide, waiting for you to receive him in your heart today. God is allowing us time every day that he wakes us up another morning to get our house in order we should use our time wisely here on earth to do the things that God has set out for us to do.

So don't wait till God is calling you, and your life has come to an end for there won't be any more time left, you can't say then when dying comes "oh please Lord allow me one more chance", and I promise I'll get it right this time. God is allowing us a chance right now there are no more excuses "today is the time to make that decision", time is winding up, and if you are not ready when dying comes then you don't stand a chance without Christ on your side. He is the only one that can solve your case on judgment day, Satan's not going to help you if you haven't excepted Christ, Satan's going to be laughing because he knows what's going to happen, and then he will be the one who has won, and waiting for you to join him, and his angels in a dying grave forever on judgment day, and there will only be one of authority and that's God he will decide where your destiny will be in Heaven or the grave. So please except Christ as your Savior today he said in his word John 14:6 No man can comes thru God except by me, and his name is Christ this is not make believe by no means for God is real so make that change before it's too late and know that if you except him today, your name will be written in the book of life, and you will live with him forever, no sickness, no sorrow, no troubles and the streets are paved with gold in his house are many mansions one for you, and there's one for me.

Just imagine a place where there's happiness every day, no suffering ever again like here on earth, aren't you tired of going through pain, and disappointment, son against male parent, female parent against daughter, no troubles no worries ever again, you never have to worry about a bill or house note because Christ, God's precious son he paid it all for us he loves us all, and those who love, and trust him will live again. So trust God with your life for it is he that is in control for God has got all the power of life and dying is in his hands.

CHAPTER 2

Don't Take Things
For Granted

There are times in my life when I didn't realize just how blessed I am considering all the things that I have been through, I fully now understand that my life could have been cut off many times, but it was by the grace of God I made it this far in my life. There are times when we take the little things in life for granted sometimes by simply not letting our family, and friends know how much we love them, to some of us we may think oh they know how I feel about them, but in reality simple words like "I love you", or showing someone how much you love them can mean a lot. There's an old saying "give me my flowers while I'm yet living" in other words show me your love while I'm still alive because when I'm deceased, and gone I'll never know you cared. I've been given a second chance to do that, it is so very important to let our friends and loved ones know how much they mean to us while they are yet living, because when they're gone we won't get a chance to say I love you, or do you know how much you mean to me, is there anything that I can possibly do for you, or I'm so sorry I didn't mean to offend you.

You never know the slightest little thing may mean so much to that person where you thought it probably didn't mean much at all, God gave me all of my siblings, there have been times when I really didn't like what some of them had to say to me, but it was for my own good to help me to enjoy a healthy life and I know now it's because they cared. Sometimes what we think is not good for us is the best thing for us, I sometimes felt that they were against me, but God reminded me in his word in Romans 8:31 If God be for us who can be against us? I remember different ones in my family would tell me that I need to eat healthy because of the fact that I am a diabetic, a lot of times I would see them eating foods that I no longer should eat too much of, you know the good tasting carb foods like peach cobbler, homemade cakes, banana pudding, the starchy foods, etc., and if I did choose to eat those foods, I would not do it in moderation, so I had to learn to discipline myself and learn to eat to live. The same thing applies to other people who may have hypertension, heart conditions or other medical problems that affect what we put inside our bodies such as fried foods, gravies, fatty or

28

spicy foods. Our bodies are the temple of the Holy Spirit, the Word says in 1st Corinthians 6:19 you are not your own you were bought with a price so we should honor God with our body.

When Christ lives in us, our bodies need to be in good health as this is what he wants for us, so that we will be able to do the things that he needs us to do. We cannot help others if we are not in good health ourselves so we should not take these things for granted, and besides you will feel so much better, and enjoy life better when you feel good. I remember before I became very ill in my body I would fail to be more aggressive in following up to make sure I told my physician what was wrong in my body or if I had a physician that I felt didn't really listen I would not change physicians so my health became worse, we can't rely on others all the time to make decisions for us, sometimes we have to be the more aggressive one to make those choices for ourselves there are times when you have to be the one to make that first step, besides if you don't take care of yourself as the old saying goes then whose going to do it for you, not always your family or friends, some decisions we have to make for ourselves, so don't take for granted that someone is going to always take care of things for you, yes at times we may get help from family, friends or other sources, but they are not the ones dealing with your health issues especially if you are in a position that you can possibly get better by eating right, exercising, or taking your medications on time, and following up with your physician appointments timely, or making important decisions when it comes to your own health, if you're already unable to do these things or make decisions for yourself then that's a different situation, but sometimes we can avoid some things from happening if we would have took time to just think, and say you know I could have perhaps avoided this from possibly happening if I would have at least tried to take better care of my health.

So don't act as if you're incompetent of making your own decisions if indeed you are capable of managing your own matters, please never take those things lightly you know some things can be avoided by simply following your physician's orders you may just save your life or the possibilities of being placed in a nursing home, or assistive living, and I'm not saying that it's a bad thing to live in those kind of institutions because sometimes you may have no choice or it may fall in your best interest or your families, believe me, I've been there, and done that, but what I am saying is learn to really do the things that may help you live as long as you can, and simply enjoy the things in life that bring joy and happiness to you, wake up and smell the coffee, and that is to say start living and not just existing, exhilarate yourself, get out go to a movie, go shopping if you have the extra money, get involved in something that will be enjoyable to you that you know is pleasing unto God. I get joy when I just even see older married couples holding hands, people taking trips together, fishing, boating, camping or going to church and being involved in your church, be happy, and enjoy this life while you have a chance. Sometimes people think you have to have a lot of money just to enjoy life, and that is far from being correct, you'll be amazed at the things in life that can be enjoyable such as just simply having a friend over just to talk and have a cup of coffee, or inviting family or friends over for a Sunday dinner or a night out at the movies with family or friends, spending time with your grand kids, nieces and nephews, siblings playing cards, or dominos, etc. there are so many ways to enjoy life, and still be pleasing in Gods eyes.

You may enjoy just getting in the kitchen and cooking a sweet potato pie or baking a cake for a friend or family member and get the enjoyment out of how much they love your cooking, paintings, drawings singing, or any gift God has given you to make someone else smile and you will be surprised how this may fill an empty space in your heart to see the happiness of others will make you happy also. See there are times if we will forget about ourselves, and do our best at putting a smile on the faces of others, you will be surprised at just how good it will make you feel. I remember when I used to take care of my nieces and nephews I now cherish those moments, and the times that I spent with them, one of my nephews joined the navy, now he and his spouse stay far away so when I get to see them

I cherish each moment I get to spend with him and his spouse so I never take those kind of things for granted anymore.

I never know when or if I will ever see them again, so don't take even the smallest things such as the smell of the summer flowers, the smell of rain, some people don't have all of their senses, and would give almost anything to enjoy these things. God has created a beautiful world he has given to man to enjoy while we are here on earth, we see it in the parks, lakes, beaches, and everywhere we go we can see beauty that our God has created, and put here on earth for us to enjoy even in the ideas that he has given man to create for us to enjoy such things as amusement parks, nice hotels, restaurants, movie studios, shopping malls, etc., so we know there has to be a God to love man so much that he would create this earth with such beauty for us to enjoy in this life as well. I think that it would be a dishonor to God to have given us such a beautiful world and the things in it, and we not take advantage of any of its many amenities that he has put here on earth for us to enjoy while we are here. We can enjoy this life, in Christ thru his way that he gives us in his Word, as my William used to say it's the basic instructions before leaving earth, and as long as we are in his word we are covered through the lamb Christ our Savior, and if we mess up, don't give up, just say Lord I messed up today, help me Lord to get it right the next time, and be sincere when you say it, and he will help you.

I am so fortunate to have overcome the obstacles in this race of life, but with God's help I'm reminded of the hymn by Donnie McClurken "We Fall Down But We Get Up", I was able to get back up again and get back into the race in which his word applied to my life, and which may apply to your life as well. This race is not given to the swift, or to the strong, but it is given to one who endures to the end. So even though we sometimes make some mistakes in life, don't give up keep trying we're going to make mistakes in this life, we're not perfect, we only strive to get there, but as long as we have life in our bodies we have a chance to get back pull ourselves together, and make it right so that we don't have to say that I should have done this or that. Each day that we can wake up and see a new day should give us the initiative to make everything right on this side of our life without having any regrets before dying comes our way, if you've offended someone say I'm sorry or I didn't mean to offend you even if you were in the right, it never hurts to be the bigger one and apologize, love one another the Word says John 15:12 This is my Commandment, that ye love one another, as I have loved you.

The most important thing of all is to ask God to forgive us for our sins, and to believe that he sent his only son to die for our sins, and ask him to come into our lives and live in us as our Lord and Savior, and if you will say this prayer and mean it from deep in your heart you shall be saved and you will never ever regret it for he promised in his word in John 3:17 For God sent not his son into the world to condemn the world; but that the world through him might be saved. Get into a good Word based church, and learn, and study God's word for these are basic instructions before leaving earth. So don't take things for granted for there is life after dying whether you spend it in heaven or in the grave a place separated from God the choice is yours. I've had the chance to witness to one family member who often had many disagreements with some of our immediate family members, and everyone that this person had disagreements with the others in the family could not figure out why she that way until that particular family member became ill, then that family member began to have a total different perspective on life, along with their change in personality with others in the family, I felt that she had made peace with God, and all the other family members that she had issues with before she left this earth, in fact that person told some of the women in the family that they would have to help with training her daughter up in the right way which I firmly believe she felt we were capable of.

So when that family member was laid to rest the expression on her face looked so at peace, and I just felt as if she had made everything alright with God before she left this world, and I know that she knew Christ in the pardon of her sins, I just want the world to realize that sometimes it's sad, but we take it for granted that we're going to be in this old world or this side of life forever, and we are not. Sometimes it takes one to be on their dying bed, to lose a love one, or maybe for some other tragedy to come about before we truly look to God, and allow him to come into our hearts, God will sometimes chasten those that he loves, but even then he gives us free will, he's not going to make us do anything we don't want to do, but he is going to give us a chance to make the right choice, remember when our parents punished us when we did something wrong not because they liked punishing us, but because they loved us so they wanted us to learn from our mistakes, well that's the same way it is with God he wants what's best for us, but he wants us to open our eyes to see it.

The good thing about it is that God still gives us his grace, and mercy, but the sad thing about it is that we sometimes take God for granted even though we know he is going to be there for us through all our miseries, and pain, but sometimes God will allow things to happen, not that he wants to see us hurt, but because he loves us so, he's the rose of Sharon, the Lily of the valley, he's the Bright, and Morning Star, he's the Lord of lord's, the Beginning, and the Ending sometimes he just needs to get our attention, and once that happens we become ready to throw up our hands, and say what will you have me to do Lord? I for one do not want to take God for granted world, he is too good of a God, and he deserves all the praise, the honor, and the glory just because of who he is. He's a healer, a deliverer, our God is an awesome God, and we should love him just because of who he is, some people treat God like he's sugar, when they get what they want, then they want to toss God to the side, please, world don't take him for granted. God loves us, if he didn't he wouldn't have sent his only son here on earth to die for our sins even when we didn't deserve it. We sometimes act as if God has to do things for us, and he doesn't, he didn't have to wake us up this morning, but he did, he didn't have to give us our health and strength, he didn't have to allow us to be covered in our right minds, but he did and we often take those kinds of things for granted such as the air we breathe, there's so much of God's goodness if I had ten thousand mouths I couldn't tell all of God's goodness.

Each time I wake up, I thank him, I could have been deceased, and in my grave, I could have been with no food to eat, or no shelter to lay my head at night, everyone has something to be thankful for, we all have something in this world that someone else may not have, so we should be grateful unto God, and even if we don't we can do something to help someone else in some kind way, even if it's just an encouraging word to someone, or sharing the love of Christ in some other way that will be a help to somebody on this earth, I remember looking at some of the hungry people on Joyce Meyers Show one day, I can remember this little African girl who had some little siblings that needed food and they had no parents to look after them, but each day she would go out to the dump grounds near the village to try and round up something to feed her family, even if there wasn't much left for her to eat, I thought here this little girl has such a kind heart that she thought more of her siblings, she had more concern for her family than she did for herself, which she could have been selfish, and just thought about herself.

I thought boy she could really teach some of us more fortunate people here on earth a thing or two about compassion for one another. Some of us are so busy and wrapped up in ourselves, or what about me as Joyce Meyer always says that we do not think for once, and ask God what would you have me to do today to be a help to somebody, even if you can just pray with a person who may be going thru something certainly if you're a believer you know prayer changes things. It is so easy to take things for granted when we are more fortunate than others because of the simple fact that we don't take the time to think that because we're hungry that God did not have to provide us with any food on the table.

God didn't have to provide us with jobs so that we could provide for our family, so many people don't have jobs, don't even have food on the table, but a lot of us do, and we just take it for granted, and fail to thank God each day, or fail to thank him for waking us up this morning, we could have been deceased, and in our grave, but God spared us to be in the land of the living another day, and none of us deserve it, but he woke us up anyway, some of us he allowed us time to get our life together to say yes to his will, to say yes, and admit we have sinned and come short of his glory, and ask him to come into our life, he spared you another day, and you still won't allow him to come into your life, and there are still some people in this world that know for sure if they were to die today they would not be ready if Christ came today, but his grace is so sufficient he allows us breath in our bodies another day, another day to get ready for no man knows the hour when the son of God comes, so it pays to be ready when dying comes our way, that there will be no reservations in our mind that we are ready when he comes. We take it for granted as if we're going to be on the face of this earth forever. I want to share this with you, God gave us all the gift of life, and it is up to you, and I to live it according to his will, and for the adoration, and building of his Kingdom Come, for we were born to worship, and praise his holy name the Word says in Psalms 150:6 let everything that hath breath praise the Lord.

Man not only takes things for granted he takes God for granted too, people act as if it's already settled that they're going to wake up tomorrow, or if their guaranteed to have a job tomorrow or be in good health, and God wants us to have all this, and good health, but we must seek him first, and all these things will be added unto you in his word, so don't take him for granted God is a good God, and he deserves better than we give him. We need to start living every day of our lives as if each day was our last day here on earth, and try to do our best to do what God has laid out and planned for each of our lives, because we all have a purpose from God for all of our lives, so when we discover that purpose which is intended in our life, then is when we need to say yes, and began to do what God wants us to do here on earth, before we leave this earth, some may say, well I don't know what my purpose is, then go to God, ask him in prayer, and if you're surely sincere in your heart he will reveal it to you.

We all have something to do to help to build God's Kingdom so it is important that we are up, and about God's business, and stop taking it for granted as if there is always going to be a tomorrow, because tomorrow is not promised, the Word says in Matthew 25:13 Watch therefore, for ye know neither the day nor the hour wherein the Son of man cometh. So we must be ready when he comes, Matthew 16:27 says when he comes he shall come in the glory of his God with his angels, and then he shall reward every man according to his works. If you haven't done any works, toward the Kingdom, then don't expect to be paid because every man will be determined accordingly. I don't know about you, but I want to hear him say well done thou good and faithful servant. This life here on earth is not to be taken lightly, Christ is coming back, and he's coming back for a church without a spot or a wrinkle, and that is to be just like him, and if we'll not just read the Word, and go to church weekly, and on Sundays, but apply the word to our lives daily, then we will be that church that Christ is coming back for. I love him world each day I want to be pleasing unto him.

Won't you let him come into your heart today, if you're not a Christian, Christ loves you my he's standing at the door knocking won't you let him in, don't allow the enemy which is Satan to still your joy, because there is joy in the Lord, some people may say well I'm having heaven right here on earth, I've got a nice house, a good job, plenty money, fancy cars, I'm enjoying things right now, but let me tell you world, those are only material things, and that will not last always, and yes there's nothing wrong with having those things, but if you have things, and you don't have Christ that's not enough, those things will perish, but if you have Christ you have a promise of eternal life with him forever what God has prepared for you no one can come and take it away like here on earth, so don't laugh it off, and take what I'm saying for granted, when dying comes Satan is not going to be in your corner, but if you've got Christ he's the only way you, and I can make it into his Kingdom, so when that day of judgment comes, and you will be reminded if you took every chance you had for granted, and never once tried to change your life while you still had breath in your body to make things right with God. Deuteronomy 30:19 says choose you this day who you will serve.

As for me, and my house we will serve the Lord. I don't know about you world, but I want to go back with him when he comes, and he will come, John 5:20 says marvel not at this, there will be a time that all the deceased who are in their graves will hear his voice, and come out, those who have done good will rise to live, and those who have done evil will rise to be condemned. It's going to be just like that old hymn I used to hear a long time ago, oh when the Lord gets ready you got to move, it tells about how momma, papa, or siblings, when he gets ready we all got to move, if you're in your grave, if you're sitting at the dinner table when he comes you're going to have to move, there's no doubt about it, just don't let him catch you with your work undone, so it pays us all to be ready, and be about God's business, because Christ is coming back soon for his bride, and that's the church, and if you're wrapped up, and covered in the red fluid of Christ that's you and me church, will you be ready world, don't take this thing called salvation lightly we've all got to work out our own soul salvation, your parents, can't do it for you, your siblings can't either, I heard some people say my dad was a preacher, or my mom used to be a Sunday school teacher that's all good, and ok but we have to work this thing out for ourselves, just because you may have been brought up in the church that's not going to get you into heaven, your parents had to work out their own soul salvation, and we do too so we must be born again, and that begins with accepting Christ into your life as your Lord and Savior, and admitting that you are a sinner, and ask Christ to come into your life, and ask him to change you, and live inside you because he is the only one who can truly change us, you can't do it yourself, but with his help, and him living inside you, and you staying in his word daily, and have a close relationship with him.

When we have a close relationship with our friends or loved ones we talk to them keep an open line of communication with them, and Christ wants the same with you, and I he wants you to talk to him, ask for his guidance in all we endeavor to do, he wants to be our friend our confidant so he has our best interest at heart. How many times have some of us in this world shared things with someone that we thought we could trust, and they let you down, not with Christ he will never let you down because he loves you, and he cares for you, and Christ has no respect of person he loves us all, and for that alone to be able to put our trust in God is something we should not take likely when you trust in someone they give you hope they give you promise, and when that happens you can expect something in return for instance as when you put your money in the bank you trust the bank with your money you feel assured that it will be safe when you need it, you can believe it will be there.

When you take your infant to the daycare you trust the daycare givers with your son or daughter you feel that your offspring will be safe, and be well taken care of, or when you go to church you trust that the minister will feed your soul with the word, and that it will be food for your soul, all these things you trust to happen, now some of these things or people could perhaps let you down, politicians sometimes promise us things, just to get them into office, or the Bank could take your money, and make up all kinds of excuses why you don't have ex amount of dollars in your account, or the daycare could put your son or daughter at risk, and something terrible happen to that son or daughter, or your minister could mislead you wrong when you put your trust in who you think is a man of God, and that all goes to say that when you find a for sure thing that won't let you down no matter what you shouldn't take it for granted because you know you can rely on it because it is a for sure thing, and that's the thing about Christ you can trust him, he'll be there, and right on time for God is good all the time, and we should never take him for granted, his grace is sufficient even when we don't deserve it that's what kind of God he is.

God loves us so unconditionally that nothing we do can stop him from loving us, my there's no love like it ever as the hymn goes I searched high, and low still couldn't find anybody, nobody greater for there is nobody greater than God is. I remember thinking back when my dad was living, and we kids would all sit around the table, and we always seem to have a full course meal on the table, and as I can remember on most Sundays my mother would always manage to cook a real nice Sunday dinner for us all. I think about how God provided for us in hard times, how much more will he provide for us now, all of us if we'll just trust him, little things like that we didn't think much of it back then until now, but God always made a way, we had clothes on our back, shelter a place to stay we never got put out, somehow dad always managed to pay the bills, I can't remember ever not one time that our lights, gas, phone or water got cut off, but because my dad was a man that trusted in God, not in his job, his friends, neighbors, or not even in what proficiency he was gifted with, but he totally trusted the one and only almighty God.

We as kids may have taken it lightly then, but now I know that we shouldn't ever take the kind of love that our God has for us for granted, he had our backs in all situations no matter what the circumstance may be nothing is too hard for him to make a way out of no way for he's a big God, a merciful and kind God, he can handle any situation no matter how big, or how small the problem may be, and we should thank him every day for he is so worthy to be praised. Psalms 150:6 says let everything that hath breath praise ye the Lord. So give God the glory, and all the honor, and never take God's goodness for granted if you're alive you could have been in your grave today, if you can see, hear, smell, taste, and feel then he has already blessed you with the basic essentials that your body needs to survive, and even if you don't have all the basics, he still loves you, and he has a purpose for all of us no matter what flaws we have in life, God can take that flaw, and hide a multitude of faults. What the enemy which is Satan meant for bad, God can turn that thing around for your good.

For he's an on time God yes he is, as the hymn goes he may not come when you want him, but he's always right on time he's an on time God yes he is. So don't take him for granted because it's not over until God says it is. I hope you receive this as God has laid it on my heart. A lot of times in the Word Christ spoke in parables, I'd like to share this parable with you there was once a man who took a woman to marry she was very kind, she would always try to please her man, but he never seem to appreciate anything she would ever do, she kept the house clean for him, kept meals on the table each day from breakfast, lunch, and dinner she even performed as most people would say her duties as a spouse, the man still never seemed to be satisfied he would always find some way to criticize her, never complimented her for all the good things she did do, but always seem to have something negative to say about her.

So one day after so many years of marriage the woman grew tired of her man's attitude toward her, and approached her man after her weeping countlessly from criticism, the man never knew not once that she cried so many times behind closed doors after being criticized so much she held the pain within her until she couldn't bare it anymore without saying something to him, so one day she asked her man why is it that you have always criticize me, so many times countlessly, no matter how hard I have tried to please you. I've tried to be a good woman keep you satisfied in every way that I could possibly think of that a woman should please her man; I know some women would have left you a long time ago if you would have criticized them the way that you have me all these years. The woman looked her man in the eye, and said you do not know a many nights as we laid in bed, I cried while you were asleep, and you never knew it because it hurt me so for you to be so critical of me, and I felt I was doing everything within me to satisfy you, but you didn't even seem to appreciate it no matter how hard I tried to please you. The woman stood there calmly waiting for a response from her spouse, finally he held his head down, he could not even look her in the eye, and he said, I have no excuse I just took you for granted. She slowly walked up to her man, and she said look at me, and the man looked up at his woman, and she said I want you to truly look at me, I know I don't look like the same woman you married years ago, but out of all those years even when the wrinkles weren't there I truly loved you, and wanted to be pleasing to you, and you say that your excuse for treating me that way is simply that you just took me for granted, well then she sighed for a moment, so I guess you did, and I forgive you for that, so the woman turned away, and said I'm going to bed now. The man sat there vaguely, and thought about all the ugly things he had said to his woman and how he had treated her so badly throughout the years, and later went to the bedroom where his woman laid there in the bed, he cut off the light, and got into bed, and he said as he laid next to her," Cora was her name", he said Cora I'm sorry If I had it to do all over again, honey I wouldn't treat you that way ever again. There was nothing but silence in the room, the man called her name again Cora did you hear me, oh I guess you're angry at me now as he made a guttural sound from his voice, the woman she said nothing he turned on the light, his woman was turned the other way he gently turned his woman by her face, and she had died. The man began crying out loud "Oh Cora I didn't mean it honey" as he held her in his arms repeating it over and over again in despair. So the morale to this story is never take anything or anyone for granted tomorrow is not promised, and it might be too late. It was too late for him to tell Cora he was sorry, but not too late to tell God that he was sorry for the way he had treated his woman and ask God for forgiveness.

A lot of times we take God for granted as if he has to put up with all the wrong things that we do, and we never say forgive me Lord, I didn't mean it, or I didn't mean to be displeasing unto you, and fail to ask for his forgiveness, and yet he is merciful time after time because he loves us just like Cora was with her man, but oh we don't want to see an angry God that has grown tired of us repeatedly taking him for granted, and then it's too late because like Cora who finally grew tired of the way her man had treated her until finally she had to do something about it, and began dying of a broken heart, so when we fail to try to make it right with our fellowman, God wants us to truly love one another, and to show that love by how we treat or talk to one another that's why we should be careful what we say for out of the mouth the overflow of the heart speaks, and it may be too late to tell someone you're sorry for life can be gone in a second. That's why Christ told us in his word John 13:34-35 to love one another even as I have loved you.

Love can truly hide a multitude of faults like Cora maybe she didn't do everything like her man thought she should have done things, but what she did do she did out of love for her man which should have been good enough for him. Cora didn't have to keep the house clean her spouse could have come home after a hard day's work as many days to a dirty house, or have to eat fast food, TV dinners, or no dinner at all, or told him at night sorry I've got a headache when it came to pleasing her man in bed. I'm sure we don't do everything as perfect as God would like us to do things, but because he knows if we love him in all that we do" God overlooks our flaws", and he teaches us in his word how to become better at what he wants us to be. Cora may not have been a perfect woman to her spouse, but if her man would have shown a little more love for his woman, and told her in a nice way what he would like her to do differently I'm sure she would have taken his judgment with a grain of salt, and she wouldn't have felt as if he was being so bitter toward her, she would not have felt as if she had been taken for granted.

So as we live our lives daily please don't fail to appreciate the little things in life, appreciate each other love one another in the things you say and do toward each other, learn to be thankful of the things God provides us with daily like our family, friends, health, the weather when we need rain, sunshine to make things grow, or the cold to freeze and destroy germs or anything that is being done for us in some kind way whether through our loved ones doing things for us or thru God doing for us. Please don't take things, for granted, and most of all don't take God for granted he's too good to us, and better than what we deserve. So never think that things are already settled, to go the way we think that things should happen, every day is not always going to be the best day, but even in the midst of the bad days you can enjoy everyday life, in a pleasing way to God, but remember in the midst of it all, don't take things for granted.

CHAPTER 3

Given A Second Chance

Life can sometimes be like a deck of cards, sometimes you're not always dealt a good hand, but if you use the hand you've got and make the best of it, take a chance you may come out a winner rather than pondering about if I could do it all differently I'm sure a lot of us would do better on the next round at least those who have become wiser. There is no mistake that God allowed me to come back to life again for such a time as this, sometimes in life we don't understand God's plans for us, we just have to remember that God is working things out for our good, and to trust him, and know that he is God, and he has it all under control like the card player you trust your partner to play his hand well, and make the right decision when playing the right card so you believe they have your back right, same way with God if we play our cards right in other words do what is right according to his word then he's got our back, but you must make the right choices because God won't honor wrong so we must make decisions in accordance with his word. As I laid down in my medical bed, I didn't really understand the dying part of my life, but as I found myself speaking to God, I remembered asking him at one point if he'd let me survive, and conquer this feeling of dying, I promised that I would make a vow, and I won't take it back, and that's usually what we say when he brings us through something like a very serious part of our storm in life, and when he does bring us thru it we sometimes don't admit that we did forget what we had promised because we are human, but when Christ was placed on the cross there is no excuse anymore on our behalf, for life has its own set time, mine and yours.

Some people besides myself have had the chance to have an out of body experience, just before God brought me back to life, I literally saw myself on a cross, everyone experiences dying differently some have been to grave, and back, some have been to Heaven, why I don't really know only God knows, we can estimate, and say maybe it's what they were going thru at that time, it may have been a test, we all are in our own individual world of hidden secrets of darkness, everyone handles their mysteries differently, while they are in their mindful memory journal of unfamiliar facts which doesn't always last long, and sometimes it may last a lifetime, to make a long story short we all are going to experience webs in our lives, things that are hidden whether they are natural or spiritual webs we get all caught up in things in this life sometimes which causes us to become blind of things you may not always foresee before you get there. Sometimes we don't know what's ahead until we get to that point, sometimes it may be too late, and we have to struggle our way through to risk that probability of fortune whether good or bad, it is our future what is to come of it is our choice. While I was on my dying bed, I was put into a place of rest, because I really didn't know how to rest, sometimes our bodies just need to rest while God is working on our souls.

We do it every day on our jobs, in our daily busy schedules, and we get so caught up in work or family that we don't take the time to take care of ourselves we just keep going and going like the Ever Ready Battery until God just puts us in a position where we have no choice but to sit down and get some rest so that we are able to finish what he has laid out for us to do. Sometimes God has to just stop us to get our attention. I was always trying to be in every place at one time and I couldn't be everywhere at every time, something was always going on at the church, over a friends, or family members place, and I would try to be there, but God made us human in his word he tells us we are destroyed because of lack of knowledge, we try to be hero's for one another, we put on our Superman or Wonder woman of armor, but instead we fail to realize God is our only hero, and if we will put on our Spiritual Amor of warfare clothing which is our whole armor garment the word of God that we need to apply to our lives to verify in our natural and spiritual walk with God, and then we will be ready for anything that comes our way. The word says in 2 Corinthians 10:4 for the weapons of our warfare are not carnal, but mighty through God to the pulling down of strong hold. In other words the weapons we struggle with are not weapons of this world, but the weapons that we have to battle with when the enemy comes our way is the word of God which has divine power, and is pleasing unto God. So when we run into problems in this life, run to the rock which is God. There were so many people that I saw coming into my room as I lay there in the medical building saying God has favored you for a second chance in life, many of them went on about how I had gone through so much, but when I was on that operating table, I felt myself literally struggling for my life back.

I can remember it very well as if it were yesterday, September 28, 2004 on a Monday morning, I remember waking up that morning after washing my face, and brushing my teeth, I walked to the kitchen for breakfast, when I opened the refrigerator door, the light lit upon my feet, and looking at my feet they seem so thick, and fat. I mean they were immensely large so I started to panic, then I felt as if I was going to faint. I remember calling Lisa to take me to the emergency room, when I asked her to take me to the medical building she said to me it's a mind thing Val so I started outrageously thinking one word, and that word was dying. So as Lisa, and I arrived in the emergency room my heart started racing in a beat that I could hear so loudly as if I had a stethoscope in my ear. So when I laid on the stretcher while the medical assistants and physicians were walking around, and verifying my fluid pressure among other things, one of the physicians saw my toes on one of my feet my left foot, there were some knats flying around it, the foot also had a dying scent to it, so the physicians took a while returning to the emergency room, so as I waited for the physicians to let me know what they were going to do, before I knew I was being prep for immediate surgery, then later the transporters began rolling away to have my surgery.

When I arrived to the area for surgery, I had to perhaps wait another half or maybe hour so I began to have a fear of dying upon me. Finally the physician came in, and just before I entered the room for my surgery the question that was asked of me was did I have any last words, and so when I heard the word last I began to have great concern, I remember as I was entering the room I remember the physician saying are you ready, my answer was yes so when they gave me anesthesia, I remember getting very sleepy, and they put the oxygen mask on my face, I remember saying the last words, I can't breathe. When I finally came to, I remember seeing three ministers of which one was my pastor. I then went into a coma, there were times that I would come out, and then I would go right back into it, the last time I went back into a coma, I started seeing others that were already deceased, now when I saw my dad I was in a place like no one but God could see me through it. No one could have survived what I had experienced without God on their side, but I know, and realize that had it not been for him I wouldn't have survived thru it all. As I can remember my physician told me he had eight physicians trying to hold me down so as I remembered that the number eight means the beginning, so God was letting me know that this is just the beginning of" my new life of a second chance".

As I lay there I felt so much like every ounce of strength had come out of me, for I had no type of strength to do anything, every time I tried to do for myself to even eat, or drink water I would repeat these words to myself, I can do all things through Christ which strengthens me, even though I was weak it was God who gave me strength. He strengthen not only my body, But my mind as well, 2 Corinthians 12:9 says for my strength is made perfect in weakness. So as I lay there in my medical bed, I began to speak to God in my heart thinking of the hymn by Marvin Sapp, "I never would have made it without you". God is so faithful, we can always count on him, man may fail us, but God won't, in Joshua 1:5 the Word says I will not fail thee, nor forsake thee, oh we have such a loving God, he is so worthy to be praised, I thank him every day for allowing me to have this second chance in life so I can tell the world how God will be right there with you no matter what you are going thru, with him by your side you're going to make it, no matter what the situation looks like he will be right there with you thru it all. We may have to go thru some struggles, some pain sometimes, but in the end you will make it he will see you thru it all, and you will look back, and know that it had to be some pain at times, but in the end you will make it he will see you thru it all, and you will look back, and know that it had to be him so God will get the glory in the end.

As I was in the medical building on September 28, 2004 I had no idea of all of the things that I had went thru in my physical body that had actually happen to me until Nora had shared with me that night, Nora was like the should have been medical assistant in the family, she was a certified aide working in Healthcare for several years, but thru all her experience as a certified aide, she paid close attention to many professional medical assistants and physicians that she learned quite a lot from them in the field of Healthcare. She asked me if I had felt some of the things that I had been going thru, and my response was no. When she told me about the many crisis that I had gone through while I was in a coma, in my mind I was so shocked, I told myself that I've gone thru all of that which was the fact that I was amazed that," I am still here". This was my confirmation that I am truly a woman of God who has been given a second chance, I even heard of other lives that had passed away even while I was going thru my transition. Many had prayed such as my family and the church even while I was going thru my transition. Many ones prayed lots of family, church family members of the Shiloh Institutional C.O.G.I.C, also members of the Potter's House in Dallas were all praying for me so there was much favor for me from the power of prayer that so many people had lifted me up before the presence of God.

James 5:16 says the effectual fervent prayer of a righteous man avails much, and 1 Peter 3:12 says for the eyes of the Lord are over the righteous, and his ears are open unto their prayers. There was so many things that had shutdown in my body, my lungs had collapsed, both kidneys had stopped working, and other parts of my body were shutting down when I was in a coma, yet out of all these other parts of my body shutting down, I was told that the physicians could not understand why everything was shutting down, but my heart was the only thing that was throbbing hard and strong, and then I remembered in his word for man looks on the outward appearance, but the Lord looks at the heart, even in that most crucial time God was letting me know that he was with me even until that most decisive moment, he was letting me know that my ending was just my beginning, even while I was experiencing this darkness of being in the valley of the shadows of dying, his word says Psalms

23:4 I shall fear no evil for he is with me, his rod and his staff were comfort for me as the days were going by so fast, he was letting me know that he would allow me this second chance, even if I didn't fully understand what all his plans were for my life, he told me to trust him, and he brought me thru, I felt as if I had been elevated to another level, so I thank God for all the prayers of the saints who celebrated in my victory of overcoming all that I had experienced, yes my family was there patiently waiting, yes the physicians worked with me through my struggle, and the saints prayed for me and I thank them all, but I owe all the glory and the honor to God, and he will reward all for their generosity of love, for having so many prayers, generosity of love, for having so many prayers, and much patience during my recovery.

There is this game we used to play called hide and seek when we were a child, and at the end we would always say ready or not, "here I come", and that's the way God is when he comes we must be ready, for no man knows the day nor the hour when Christ is coming back, he's coming for a church without a spot or wrinkle, I was given a second chance to help others to get ready for the coming of Christ thru ministry, and I strive daily in some way to do that for this is my goal to help with sharing the love of Christ to others. You know when I think about the favor on my life, it's like a gift that God has given to me, and I want to use that gift to spread joy to others to give others a chance for God to use them in a mighty and miraculous way, because believe it or not our God is so awesome that he has enough gifts to spread abroad to everyone here on earth to share in helping to spread the gospel to one another to tell of the goodness of Christ, in building his kingdom so that we can be ready when he comes, and to complete all that God wants us to do, so it should behoove everyone to not only be ready but, to stay ready and have your house in order, and when I say house I mean your spiritual house which is your soul, so that you too may be ready to go back with him when he comes, he says in his word he's going to prepare a place for us, eyes haven't seen nor ears have heard neither have entered into the heart of man the things which God has prepared for them that love him. So get things right with your parents, parents get things right with your families, and friends get things right with each other co-workers, associates all of us must love one another he said even as I have loved you. Don't put things off for tomorrow, for tomorrow is not promised to any of us so what is lacking in any of our lives we must do it while we have breath, and the red fluid is warm flowing in our bodies, our opportunity is now! Christ is waiting with his arms stretched out wide, waiting on you.

Revelations 3:20 says behold I stand at the door, and knock if any man hear my voice, and open the door, I will come in to him, and will sup with him, and he with me, God wants to give you a second chance today, you may not have the chance like I did, but he's allowing you a chance now while you have life in your body to get it right, you may have not gotten things right in the past, but Christ is allowing us that opportunity today, it's your choice he gives every man free will, salvation is free, it doesn't cost you a thing, but it will cost you your soul, if you choose to remain in a life of sin, God loves you, don't worry about any flaws you may have, I heard Kirk Franklin once say to a young man that was leading a choir, and he stutter when he spoke, so Kirk told him how he used to stutter also, but God changed that, and turned that thing around for his good, only Christ can change that, not man, but it is up to me, and other Christians to let others know that God loves you, and if you'll allow him to come into your life, he will show you the way, through his word, read it, meditate on it, he will speak to your heart, and lead and guide you daily, when we were babies we had to learn to crawl before we walked, that's the way it is when you are babes in Christ so get in a good Word based church, and stand on his word, and it's by his word that he will see you thru, so don't allow the enemy Satan to take your chance to go back with Christ when he comes, and make Heaven your eternal home, the grave was not made for man, but was made for Satan and his demons. I beg of you to except Christ today, let him come into your heart, he's waiting and knocking at your door, won't you please let him in today, he'll give you too "that second chance".

Will you except Christ today, don't say I'll do it tomorrow or next week, for tomorrow may very well be too late, Christ is standing with his arms wide open, he's waiting for you to make the first step, excepting him into your life, admitting that you have sinned, and done wrong, you make the first step, and he will do the rest, and if you ask him he will come into your heart, and make you whole again, he is the potter, and we are the clay the potter wants to give you that second chance, and put you back together again, you can't be too messed up or too broken up for Christ no matter what you have done, he still loves you, and he is waiting for you to except him today. Someone may say well I don't know what to do, or what to say, just "say yes" to his will, for it is his will that we live forever in his kingdom with God, all you have to do is say yes, and Christ will do the rest if you'll just let him into your heart today, he's waiting to give you that chance. That chance to enter into his Kingdom, that chance to become an heir to what is rightfully yours and mine, if you will just except Christ as your Savior.

Don't give up your chance to go to Heaven and be in a place where there is no more suffering, no more sorrow for eternity, because it will certainly be forever suffering, tormented by demons and sorrow in the grave, a place where there is no escape you will burn, and be in torment forever. Such a place is not meant for us from the beginning it was meant for Satan and his demons. Christ is the only one we can go through to be with God in Heaven, and if we don't have Christ on our side we don't stand a chance of making it to Heaven, for there will be only one of authority and that is God, and we need Christ on our side for he is the only one who can win our case when that time comes, and that time will come one day so don't bother to say that you didn't know, you never had a warning there are opportunities after opportunities for us all to be given a chance to make Christ our personal Savior if we fail to except him today it's nobody's fault but yours or mine. Christ is waiting on us he gives us free will of choice it has to be our decision to make that change, whether we make that change to except him or not he will still love us even until you enter the gates of the grave if that is your choice. Please except Christ today just pray this prayer, and say Lord forgive me for I have sinned and I believe that you gave your life for me on the cross, please come into my life and change me, mold and make me into the person that you would have me to be Amen. If you prayed that prayer or a prayer similar to that it's just that simple by just simply to except Christ, and ask him to come live inside of you. Get into a good Word based church, study his word, and apply it to your life daily, be baptized, and filled with God's Holy Spirit.

When you except Christ your name is written in the Book of Life! I am so glad I made that choice one day of excepting him into my life, and I'm so grateful that I have been given this chance to help win souls to Christ, just think how great it would make you feel to know when you get to heaven that you were responsible for someone's life changing for the better, and because you told that person about Christ and you ministered to them that you will see that person or others in heaven which helped them to become saved as well, and kept them from a dying grave, and a life of torment in the grave forever. Just imagine being in a place where there is no more illness, no pain, no poverty we won't ever have to worry about the economy for there will be no need to economize Christ paid it all on Calvary on the cross. There'll be no more sickness, you won't need Obama Care, Heaven is free of heartache, sickness, and pain you'll never have to worry about anyone being mean to you, or hurting your feelings, there will be nothing but love there. I don't know about you, but I'm looking forward to that chance to be with Christ one day so don't you want to go to a city that's not made by hand, a city where the streets are paved with gold, a city some place that God has designed just for you and me, what he has for you is for you, and what God has for me is for me, we all will be paid according to our works so we must be about our God's business daily because time is winding up. We've got to be bold as Christians and not stay in our comfort zone and worry about what people will say about us, Christ said in his word if you'll be ashamed of me, I will be ashamed of you before God. While I was in a coma there was one of the elder women of the church who was like an angel walking with me, and telling me some things about myself that I feared as a challenge she informed me that I had been in a place called Latter Bar place of bondage I would always stay in my comfort zone rather than express my emotions for fear of what others would say or think of me, it was as if I were an adult with this infant mentality inside of me afraid to speak up, and boldly say what God had given me to say.

We must all overcome fear at one point in life, she let me know that I had to go beyond being afraid, to speak up and boldly express my inner thoughts that God had revealed to me. She told me that I had to go beyond my fears and become free, not burdened by discomfort or awkward feelings of which at times would cause me to have anxiety onset which caused further illness in my body, that's one reason we shouldn't worry, stress ourselves out, we should leave those kind of things into God's hand, and let him handle the situation for us. God loves us, and he doesn't want us stressing because of our circumstances, he wants what's best for us, the good life, and how can we have a good life if we're stressed out all the time. We must trust in God it is to him from where our help will come from so we must be in expectations daily, and expect God to move in our lives miraculously. I have been given a second chance to speak with boldness when it comes to speaking on God's behalf, and boldly stand on his word, in his word he said if you lose your life for my sake, you will gain it back again that's his promise to us, and God is not a man that he should mislead us, if God said it in his word then it's final no ifs, ands, or buts God's word is precise.

So I was given this chance to overcome my fears, to speak boldly, and realize that God's got my back even if I lose my life, I will stand on his word because I know that it will pay off in the end, I am a soldier and Christ is my captain so I will run on in the army of the Lord, if I die let me die in God's army. God is such a good God, many fail to realize how good he is, he not only gave me a second chance he's given many others a second chance, some have lived thru car accidents, thru critical diseases, firearm wounds, you name it God has blessed a lot of us to see another day, some of us may not even realize when dying was at our door, and we didn't even know it, or see it coming but he spared us, he gave us another day, and another day to get it right, and some of us just live from day after day as if we think we're going to live in this world forever.

We must get ready to meet our maker, God is getting us ready for that great day, he's allowing us time to get it right before dying comes knocking at our door. So what if we've been given a bad deal of life's ups, and downs don't have a pity party with yourself get up, and make the most of it with what God has given you taking one day at a time, and make the best of it if you'll make one step God will do the rest, some of us tend to feel sorry for ourselves one thing about life is there is always someone in a worse situation than you are, but somehow if that person did not give up, and looked to God from which their help would come from then they made it thru the situation then so can you, and I, but we have to make an effort things don't always just happen we have to get to work to make things happen and ask God to lead and guide us along the way in all that we endeavor to do nothing is always going to come easy, but with determination, and perseverance you can make it thru your storm in life. God will be there right with you every step of the way if you trust in him he did it for me, and I know he'll do it for you for you are his and he cares for you. So the gift God has given us use what he has given you, and make the best of it, and with his help you will become victorious we have a chance now to get it right with God there are no more excuses we must be about God's business he's given me, and he's given you another chance, each day that we wake up each morning he's giving you a chance to get it right this time so play your cards right, don't lose your turn to get things right before you leave this world you can't do it on your own, but with God's help you can make it for Christ will carry you thru.

Christ loves you no matter what you have done in the past, Christ will forgive you he'll clean you up and wash your sins away he's ready with open arms when you are, so don't let it be too late for you, we've been given this opportunity to live an eternal life with

Christ, he's preparing a place for us right now your eyes haven't seen nor ears have heard the good things that God has in store for those who love the Lord, so the only thing we have to lose if we don't receive Christ as our personal Savior is eternal life with God. I would rather chance making it to heaven than punishment in a lake of fire in a burning grave where it is so hot there is no air to breathe you will be tormented by demons, scary things there you can't even imagine, so dark you can literally can feel the darkness, and you have no friends there no one to turn to only torment from Satan's demons. I've been given a second chance, don't lose your last chance to "make Heaven, your home".

CHAPTER 4

Enjoy Life!

I once heard that you should live life completely so that when dying comes like a thief in the night then it has nothing left to take. We need to enjoy, and live life to its full potential leaving no regrets behind, sometimes in life we do have some regrets, and we find ourselves saying I wished I had never made that mistake, or if I could do it all over again, I would do this or I would do that. People of God let's not take this gift of enjoying life for granted, we share and compare all of our life of disappointments, and our sad stories with one another, and we fail to realize how good God has been to us even though we do not deserve it, we have made mistakes over and over again, and God still forgives us, but if we do things his way there won't be any mistakes because at no time will there be any regrets ever. Doing things our way may lead to destruction, but yet God continues to give us favor, and believe me favor is not fair and yet he gives us his grace which is sufficient more than enough of what we deserve.

I would sometimes practice in my mind what I was going to say to God, when he already knew just what I was thinking, he knows our heart, and he knows when we are truly sorry about mistakes we have made, and when we are sincere about making a change for the better, and God wants what's best for us, we might not realize what's best for us but he does. Sometimes we just need to take a good look at ourselves and ask God to reveal his will for our lives to us so that we can fulfill our purpose here on earth that he has in store for us so that we will waste no time here on earth being unhappy, You see each of us the day that we were born we came into this world for a purpose, it is up to us to find out what that purpose is. Once we find out what that purpose is we must began to carry out that purpose. God has a set plan for each, and every one of us, and his plan includes a way for us to prosper in life if we will push ourselves to get to that point where he wants us to be, what God has for us we have to go after it, don't just sit and wait for things to happen, you have to get a move on so that things will start happening which is being about God's business, and start enjoying your life now, and making every minute count to contribute to the purpose for which you were meant to do in this life.

So don't allow the enemy "Satan to still what belongs to you", grab at it you have to go after your dreams go take what is rightfully yours it's already in God's plan you just have to go for it, start stepping into to your destiny, and that is to live your life to the full, and fulfill the purpose that you were meant to do while you are still here on earth, don't leave anything hidden what God has given to you, what he's given you to do no one else can do it better than the talent he has given to you if you will use that talent. Some people may say I don't know what my purpose is, then just ask God to reveal it to you, and what gift he gives you that will take your least amount of effort to do is what he has given you to do some people have the gift of teaching, singing, drawing, writing, inventing, the list goes on, and on God has enough for all of us, and some that we will probably never see or hear of simply because our God is that awesome, he is such an amazing God, and some won't even dare to use what he has given them to do. One thing you don't want is trying to copycat what someone else is good at if God hasn't given you that gift.

So enjoy life while you're here on earth thru the gifts that he has planted inside of you, and enjoy it while you are doing it whether it be with your family, friends, or other people, live for today because tomorrow is not promised, don't set back and ponder over what could have been, ask God to help you along the way of fulfilling your purpose here on earth he will open doors that no man can open if you will just trust him, and let him use you. We can enjoy life as Christians and, "enjoy life to the fullest", as long as we are in Gods will, and to be in his will is to remain in his word. I never realized how important life is until I faced a near to dying experience myself, I want others to know that God gave us life as a gift so we should think highly of the impact that our lives can leave on others in this world that are left behind if we fulfill our purpose here that God has laid out for each of us. So we should live our life as a legacy to others so they will know what it means to really live a fulfilled life in Christ. I remember coming up as a daughter my parent was a minister, and even though he was a man of God, and he stayed so busy with his ministry, and work, he still always took the time to enjoy things in life with his family, he didn't have that many boys, but he sure had a lot of girls, and he would always take out time with his girls, and dad would take all of us girls to the lake to go fishing before he had any sons that were big enough, and he would show us girls how to cut & gut a fish, he even taught us how to put a worm on the hook for bate just simple things like that most other girls dad probably never showed their daughters how to do, and some people may think well that's not the kind of things that you would teach girls to do, only boys do those kind of things, but you never know how such things simple things in life may help a son or daughter further in life. It may help them later to know how to fish with their spouse later in life, or take their son or daughter fishing who knows.

My sibling once saw a chef on television that didn't even know how to cut a fish and she was trying to win ten thousand dollars at that time, just think of what something that simple would have meant to her right then at that moment. Our dad would always find ways to help his family enjoy life, we would often go on family trips together, or at times have Sunday dinners if not at our home we went to someone else's house. My dad even made some things in the church fun, he would let us participate and get involved in things at the church so that we would not get bored, and become as some people would call it a bench member. I had forgotten about those things until after he was deceased, and now I look back at the way he lived, he left a legacy behind for his offspring to enjoy life, not so much as just with material things, but the spiritual things as well, and that's where the vivacity of life comes in. Each day I wake up one day is as challenging as the other to make my life worthwhile and fulfilling, as the hymn goes this is the day that the Lord has made, I will rejoice and be glad in it. I do realize that every day is not going to always be the same but sometimes we ought to just say Lord I thank you even thou I'm going thru hard times, financially, things aren't going well on my job, son's or daughter's aren't behaving like they should, but Lord I thank you anyway because I know that joy is coming in the morning, I know that trouble don't last always, and know that you've got my back because you're a God who cares, and I know you care for me.

So we must put our best foot forward we have to make the most out of this gift of life that God has given us, and thru all the obstacles keep on trusting in him We're going to have some ups and downs in life, but I am saying to make an effort to not let the enemy which is Satan still your joy, pray without ceasing, pray when things are good, and pray when things are not so good, and leave it in the hands of God, let him handle all your troubles, as the old gospel hymn goes take your burdens to the Lord, and leave them there. That was one of my dad's favorite hymns when he was alive; one verse of the hymn said if you trust and never doubt he will surely bring you out, take your burdens to the Lord and leave them there. He trusted God and knew that God had his back, our God he doesn't want us to worry about anything.

I remember there were times that I would stay in my room all depressed, and craved for attention from others like crazy, I wanted others to feel sorry for me because I was handicap and I thought because of that everyone should stop their everyday way of living and concentrate on mine when all along it was me who should have been considerate of them, and not want them to up and feel sorry for me, but I needed to get up and get out of that depression mood that

I had not yet been delivered from, and not want my family to treat me like a handicap but like an individual.

One day I realized I was only making myself unhappy others were still living their lives going to and fro about their daily business, and simply enjoying life and here I was drowning in my own sorrow, thinking about poor me, and the life that I Valerie Graham had missed out on, I mean I was just having a good old fashioned pity party, with just me, and that's when God spoke to me and, I said huh, you know there are times when we need to keep our inner ear that spiritual ear open so when God speaks to us we can hear, and he spoke to me again, and he said are you ready now to live, and enjoy life as I have it planned for you? Right then I began to get up, and get out and, start living again and enjoying the life that I had to live I had to stop, and take a deep breath and enjoy the life that God gave me.

So when someone in my family said they were going somewhere I didn't wait for them to ask me did I want to go, I ask them could I go, or I made it my business to come around others more often, and not sit in my room isolating myself from others, I started to call around and get a ride to church, or go outside with my nephews and nieces get some fresh air, see people smile again, have some fun, I started to enjoying life again. I began smiling more, laughing more, some people don't realize how much of a joy you'll get when you just start getting up and, making an effort to help your own self feel better, remember the hymn by Donald Lawrence and the Tri-City Singers "Encourage Yourself", we as Christians sometimes we wallow in our sorrows too much, sometimes you just have to get up and encourage yourself, and if that's what it takes to make you start feeling better, then so be it, start making someone else feel happy also, forget about self and think about someone else for a change, as Clint Eastwood would say in the movie say "make my day", I would stop and think well I'm not as bad off as I thought I was after you have talked to someone else, and find out they had worse things going on with them than you had, but yet they were still smiling. You know sometimes we never know what a person is going thru until we've talked to them, and get interested in something besides our own selves for a change we get so wrapped up into self that we forget about others, and how the next person is feeling.

Enjoy this life that you have now, don't sit down, and wait for things to happen, "get up and make things happen" if God has enabled you to. You've got to make a step, if you'll make one step God will make the next, we have to get a move on in being about our God's business, it's not going to happen sitting around moping all the time, you know Jessica Reedy her hymns are so inspirational to me, I was listening one day to one of her newest hymns called "Put it on the Altar", and that's just what a lot of us need to do is take our burdens to the Lord and leave it there.

Let God handle it if you've got a bad relationship going on, financial problems, problems on your job, no matter what it may be there is no problem that's too big for God to handle, we can't handle them, and there's no use in trying, but if we ask him to fix it, God he cares and loves all his children, but we have got to ask him, and trust him first, if you need more faith, if you need more wisdom, ask him the word says in Matthew 7:7 Ask, and it shall be given you, seek, and ye shall find; knock, and it shall be opened unto you. So we have to ask, don't be afraid, that's your God in heaven, the Word says in Hebrew 4:16 says let us therefore come boldly unto the throne of grace that we may obtain mercy, and find grace to help in time of need. Sometimes you never know what will happen unless you ask, John 16:23 says whatsoever ye shall ask God in my name which is Christ, he will give it you so ask it in Christ name, and that's your stamp to get it up there to God in prayer.

God wants us to enjoy life, and have things just as people who aren't saved, besides he owns it all, God just leant it to man for a little while and he wants you, and I to enjoy and have nice homes, cars, good finances, etc. No matter what our hearts desire he will give it to us as long as we abide in him, and his word abides in us. Our God is a good God all the time. I began thinking on some of the things in my life that I thought I wanted, but I realized later that those things in my previous life weren't the right things for me, and it was not what God had for me. I was still young, and I wanted to have a male companion but, it seem as if the relationship was going down the hill to nowhere, sometimes we have to pay the price to enjoy things of the world if it is not of God, but if it is of God there will be no price to pay, because what he has in store for us will last, that's why he said to seek ye first the kingdom of God, and his righteousness, and all these things will be added unto you.

So if you want a spouse don't go out looking for one on your own, ask God and he will send you the right man, or vice versa if you're a man ask God, and he will send you the right woman, but seek him first, and don't go looking at the first Tom or Jane that comes your way that may not be the right one for you, if that man doesn't respect you, and you're a woman, or he never shows you any kind of attention to let you know that he's truly interested in you because if he's interested in the right way he'll show you in some kind of nice, way, such as he may send you flowers, write a poem for you or something that would make you happy in a respectful way, and make sure he or she believes in going to church, and loves the Lord. The Word says in 2 Corinthians 6:14 Be ye not unequally yoked together with unbelievers, for what fellowship hath righteousness with unrighteousness?

You also have to pray, and ask God to show you, and reveal to you if he is the right one, and God will reveal it to you. I've often seen some of my siblings go thru things in their relationships that caused them pain, and I would ask myself, well or you sure you want to go thru all that pain, and misery just to be with just anyone, so I began seeking God because it didn't work out my way, the relationship just went nowhere, but even in the midst of wanting a mate someday, I had to learn to love myself first of all because I know God doesn't want me to be stuck in an unhappy relationship so that meant I had to let go of the old me and stop taking seconds, sometimes women and men you sell yourself too short by just taking the first man or the first woman that comes along, and that may not be the right mate for you, but if you'll seek God first, and let God send you the right one, he'll send you the best, and while I'm waiting I can still live as a virtuous woman, fix myself up for me, and still enjoy life, and God showed me that it didn't take a man to bring me joy in my life, God gave me joy, that inner peace, and happiness that no physical man could ever do, you can have a man, and still not be happy, but when you've got Christ he's more than enough for he'll take away all the sorrow, hurt, and the pain, and he'll make you brand new in him, he'll open your eyes to a lot of things that you would not ordinarily see with the plain eye, when you have a relationship with God he will show you stuff that you would not have even imagined on your own, and because he shows it to you it's a for sure thing, and you can best believe in it because he's not a man that he should deceive us.

So trust in God and you will be able to enjoy the life that he has given you, and your life will be so grand, and fulfilled that others will wonder what kind of God are you serving, and say boy I want some of what you've got, and they can have it in Christ if they'll let him be the center of their life, and I'm not saying it will be great every day because the enemy gets angry when he can get a peek into your future. So when the enemy Satan tries to interfere, and set a trap when God blesses you, and things are going so wonderful, the enemy is angry, and will try to make all kind of things happen to block your blessings, but just remember that trouble don't last always, just keep trusting in God, and when it's over you're going to come out better than you were before, remember Job earlier as I talked about how God gave him double for all his trouble.

So you're going to come out shining like a star when it's all over, because God is good, and he's good all the time! I just love him so, and I couldn't have such a joyous life without him, and he'll do the same for you. Sometimes in life we learn that if we had done some things differently we would have been much happier, but we have to learn thru the mistakes in life sometimes that we made, and if we would have put God first, and ask for his advice, and direction in the decisions that we made things would have turn out much better, God wants us to have that inner personal relationship with him, he'll be our advisor so when we involve him in our decisions in our everyday lives we will make the right decisions, and things in our lives will go so much smoother as to where we will be able to enjoy life better. I remember one of my siblings was really going thru some hard times in one of her relationships, but she didn't listen to the things that our dad tried to teach us about the right way about living with a man was to be married, and not shack up with a man he was trying to avoid us as his sons, and daughters to not get hurt later down the line in life. If a man truly loves you, my dad would say he will marry you, and wait on you before having an intercourse in a relationship, he will respect you, but since that sibling didn't listen she experience a lot of heartache and pain in the relationship of which my dad was trying to teach us to avoid unhappiness because he wanted his sons, and daughters to enjoy life in the right way.

God wants us to enjoy life but in the right way, his way by his word, and not our way. Our way of living will never make us completely happy, we may feel like we are happy for a while, but if it's not God's way it will backfire every time so if we seek God first then he will send us someone, and they will be the right one for us. So often we want to choose who we want to choose for our soul mate because maybe perhaps that person is so cute or so fine and good looking to us, but everything that's good looking is not always the best thing for us, and I know to some of us those qualities may be our requirements in a person that we want to live the rest of our lives with, and if that is so and our hearts desire just ask God he will give you the desires of your heart if you will put him first.

We have such a loving God he wants us to be happy, and we can be happy when we do things his way, like my dad wanted for his sons, and daughters to be happy that's the way it is when you have a dad that you know loves you, and God truly loves each and every one of us. God also wants us to enjoy life in many other ways not just in the daily relationships we have with one another, but also what we do on our jobs don't you think that God wants us to enjoy what we do every day he doesn't want us to be stuck on a job that we're not happy at doing, and if you are working somewhere that you are not happy at just ask him to bless you with something that you're good at, a promotion or ask him to bless you with a job somewhere that you will be happy, and he will if you will seek him first he's our God, and a good dad wants what's best for his sons, and daughters because that's what kind of God he is a good God all the time. I sometimes will enjoy the small things in life that God has given us such as just sitting around the house at times talking with one of my family members or a friend over the phone asking how are they doing, or making them laugh over the phone in a happy conversation, or playing gospel hymns and everyone joining in to listen, and clap to the music, it is so many ways God has given us to enjoy life that is pleasing unto him, and we should take advantage of the many things that's he has given us.

He gave us talents to use to not only make us happy, but to help put a smile on the face of others in this world. Our gifts are not given to us for only our own benefit when we use the gifts God has given us to help someone else he will increase your gift, and give you another so now you have two talents, and there are times when God expands your gifts depending on how many you can handle our God is such an awesome God he may give me two talents, and then someone else five talents depending on how well you use that talent. There are some God blesses with talents and they won't use that talent, so he will give it to someone that will use it so don't lose out on your blessings, enjoy what God has given you, and make the best of it for he has prepared a way for us on this earth to be successful at the gifts he gives us while we are here on earth to fulfill the purpose which we were born to do.

We should be so thankful as Christians for the life he has given us as his sons, and daughters we have such a fulfilling life for spreading love of Christ, and the life he has given us which makes our lives full of joy, and happiness because Christ lives within us so everything we do or accomplish in life, we feel so much better than a person who is not saved. in other words a sinner may live the good life of wealth or fame, but there's always going to be something missing, no matter what material things they have, they don't have that inner peace, and joy that we have whether we have those material things or not we'll always be at peace because we know God will take care of us, and we're rich already because our God in heaven owns it all, so if the rich man has those material things he's still bound not to be happy even with all the money he has at some point in his life because he doesn't have that inner peace, and joy which God gives us on the inside, and that is worth more than money ever can buy.

This joy we have the world didn't give it, and the world can't take it away. The real joy in enjoying life is living it as a faithful Christian, applying the word of God to your life daily, living it twenty four seven, and not just on Sunday, but seven days of the week, setting an example for the world so they too will want to live the life that we live for Christ, as I said earlier the world is looking for something different. Each day we should become better, and better at this life as a Christian, we ought to not go to the places we used to go, we ought not talk the way we used to talk, we ought to not dress the way we used to dress, and we may not be perfect, but thank God we're not where we used to be. Some people may say dress, we'll what's wrong with wearing what you want to wear, because when you were of the world you may have dressed a certain way which may be inappropriate, but when you become changed God will teach you what to wear his Holy Spirit will lead and guide you in everything that you do, and if you're going the wrong way about something the Holy Spirit will persuade you, and you will have to confess, and say forgive me Lord for that was not the right thing to do, the Holy Spirit will be a comforter, it may even lead you to go and apologize to someone, sometimes even if you were right about something God's Holy Spirit will remind you to just leave it in his hands, and God will work on that person, and change them, we can't so where we can't God will.

I remember there were times when I would say something to one of my siblings, and I really felt that I was right about what I had told them, but the Holy Spirit would speak to me to apologize, I knew I was right, but I could not change the way that person felt so I left it in God's hand to take care of the situation, and he worked it out for my good. God wants us to enjoy life so we have to start by living our lives in that which is pleasing unto to him, and that is to start by loving one another the way that he loves us. God has plans for all our lives, yet in the midst of his plans he wants us to enjoy our lives while we are here so he gave all of us gifts that would help to make the next person's life more enjoyable, for instance when we put smiles on hurting people's faces this pleases God, and it gives you a good feeling that you were able to make that hurting person smile, laughter is always good for the soul within.

If God has given you a gift to make people laugh use that gift for his glory, you don't have to use profanity, or do inappropriate things to make people laugh, just ask God to use you, and teach you what to say that would be pleasing unto to him, the same thing if you have a talent to sing, you don't have to use inappropriate language when using your gift God will open doors for you that is unimaginable if you will just trust him. So we should use our gifts to the glory and honor of God, and he will provide the way for us so that we can enjoy using the gifts that he has given us to help others in some way. I thank God for family, and friends in my life that help me each and every day to enjoy life in many ways many times my family we get together and have fun with each other simply enjoying the company of one another laughing, playing, eating and having a good time with one another. Sometimes I even share fun moments with my church family, or other friends doing things enjoyable together, and that are pleasing unto God.

This is such an amazing life that God has given us to enjoy with one another while we are here on earth, we can live a joyous life in Christ, and enjoy the life that he's given us to the full. It is so important to me that I have family around a lot, it's such an inner feeling of comfort to know that you have people around you who you know care about you especially if you are blessed to have a family like mine, one thing about our family we believe in hugs and greetings in a nice way toward other's and our family it is such a gratifying feeling to be around such a loving, and caring family as the one I am blessed to have which really helps you enjoy life when you're around people that you know who have a caring heart for others. I'm so blessed to have that in my life a family like mine, our parents are responsible for a lot of that in the way they brought us up to be loving toward one another, and they taught us a lot about the love of Christ so we can't help but to have some of that love instilled inside of us.

Each day I feel so blessed because a lot of families don't have that kind of thing we call love in their hearts for one another. Life is so much more enjoyable when you have nothing, but love surrounding you, love will hide a multitude of faults, and a lot of us have faults, but if we have love for our fellowman and for each other the love in a person's heart overrides their faults about them. Sometimes a person can really kind of get to you if they have some unlikeable ways about them, but when that same person does a lot of good toward others, and is always doing something to help someone else or put a smile on someone else face besides their own, then you can really look at that person, and say well you know they may have their ways at times, but they sure do a lot for others so you can just override that fault, and look at the kind heart in that person and it just makes them shine above their flaws, and all you can see in that person is Christ. And not saying that to be judgmental because none of us are perfect we all have flaws, but thru God's grace, and his mercy on us he looks beyond what man sees for God looks at the heart. So when you've got a good heart for your fellowman you can't help but to enjoy life because it makes you happy seeing others happy, and when we make others happy they can see Christ in us, and this will draw people in, and they will want to share the joy that you have, this is what brings souls in to Christ to lift up the name of Christ in all we can, he said in his word John 12:32 If I be lifted up from the earth I'll draw all men unto me. When we help the needy, feed the hungry, minister to the lost then we are doing our part to help others to enjoy life also.

CHAPTER 5

Exhale And Live Again

None of us could imagine how Christ must have felt after all the suffering he did on the cross for our sins, he inhaled and took it all on our behalf, I can imagine if he exhaled before he was deceased knowing that this was soon to pass, and he would soon rise again from dying on the cross. So just remember the next time as you go through your trials and tribulations in this world, just take a deep breath, and know that this soon will pass. While I was on the operating table, I didn't know if I would be able to inhale or exhale life again in my body, some people that have gone thru what I did they didn't make it, nor did they receive the opportunity that I did. I am truly blessed because I have been given another chance to live my life again to exercise the gift that God has given me in this life so that when I have finished running this race of life then, and only then will I exhale from this tedious journey with relief knowing that I have done all that God in heaven wants me to do, and I can hear him say well done thy good and faithful servant in the end.

Some of us don't take this life seriously we take it like we're going to be here forever we are only passing through this way of life for a short period of time, we will hear no name or number called when it becomes our time to leave this world, we must be ready at all times while we are yet alive. The Word says in Matthew 24:36 but of this day and hour knows no man, no, not the angels of heaven, but God only. Matthew 24:44 says Therefore be ye also ready for in such an hour as ye think not the son on man cometh. So I think it behooves us to be ready when Christ comes, we should consider how God allows us to experience this gift of life, and we should live it each day as if it were our last time here on earth, we must strive daily to make it an earnest effort to make heaven our home, I consider it a privilege just to be here in the land of the living to see family, and friends none of us knows when dying may come our way.

Many of my family members, and others are facing all kinds of challenges in their lives, some are experiencing so much hurt, pain and discomfort or family disagreements which is usually in every family at some moment, which makes it hard I understand at times to live with, and causes many of us to exhale loudly after being so frustrated with them, but yet we sometimes need one another so we just let out this audible breath, and endure till the end of our decisive moments, and not allow them to have that kind of effect on us, and just live our lives as God would have us to enjoy life and one another, and stop being so indignant against one another.

There are enough concerns now days with the economy being so bad, than for families to linger on the petty things in life or anyone for that matter to dwell on things that are merely relatively unimportant. My goal and all of our goals should be to make a change in this life of ours as Michael Jackson's hymn would say take a look at the man in the mirror, and make that change. Out of all the scarcity in life of loved ones and other people living in poverty, we must take care of God's business, and he will take care of ours, Mark 14:7 says for ye have the poor with you always, and when so ever ye will ye may do them good: but me ye have not always. This is a part of our purpose here on earth to be a help to others, and have joy in doing so even if it is as simple as making someone smile, feeding someone, offering to help someone stranded on the side of the road, we all need each other, people across the land have needs, and God wants you and I to help to make a change in this world, yes God himself has the power, but that's why he created man in his own image so that we would represent him, we are his hands, his servants and we should be dedicated to please God for the purpose that he has for us, we should be forever indebted to God for he gave his only begotten son for our sins, God was so displeased with man in Galatians 4-5 speaks about how God sent the spirit of his son into our hearts so that we may become heirs also, and receive the same benefits as sons and daughters, and not slaves of sin.

God wants what's best for us as his sons, and daughters, sometimes we think that we have things all figured out so we want to do things our way, and not God's way, but if we'll just trust him and admit that we've fallen short of the glory of God, and do things his way, and not make the wrong decisions by handling or doing things our way, the Word says in Isaiah 55:8 For my thoughts are not your thoughts, neither are your ways my ways, said the Lord. So we want to question is God's way easy, which in all is free from anxiety or pain, and here God is saying our ways uneasy, and so then we go and get ourselves in an uncomfortable situation, and then later after we realize the consequences from the choices that we make, we want to come and unload our burdens to God, and if we would have done things his way in the first place we would have saved ourselves a lot of trouble and heartache, and being the merciful forgiving kind of God he is, God forgives us anyway, and gives us grace for his grace is sufficient even though we don't deserve it.

His grace is not something that we can work to earn, God is such a good God he has such love for us even when we do wrong he still forgives us, and allows us another chance to get it right. When

I came back from out of my coma, God allowed me to breathe again this life of mine, I had once inhale all these frustrations into my life which kept me from gratifying to do the things that God had put me here on earth to do. Sometimes we will let things in this life have such an ill effect on us we become so frustrated that we let those things become a stumbling block to us, and we forget our purpose or goal to get those things that we want accomplished in life, and instead we give up instead of asking God to help us, that's why it's so important to allow God to guide us in all we endeavor to do in this life so that we will be successful in accomplishing our dreams, our goals in life. So once again God breathed into my nostrils, and I can exhale and live again, when I eat, to live so that I may perhaps turn this disease of diabetes around in my favor, instead of feeling sorry for myself, I think of what I can do to help others, and I enjoy life, and I encourage others to do the same. Take care of your bodies, spend time with your family, and friends, live in the will of God, you will enjoy life and it will be more satisfying knowing you lived your life here on earth to the full, and knowing you will be rewarded in heaven simply because you made a change for God's kingdom, and you did it while you were here on earth. Wouldn't it bring such joy to your heart to know that because of you somebody was saved from a burning grave, and they won't have to spend eternal life in the grave, because of something you did or said that made a change in their life, or lifestyle that was not pleasing in the sight of God, but because of you a difference was made in someone else life for the better.

When we take care of God's business he will definitely take care of ours, life can sometimes become uncomfortable because of the choices we make in our walk with Christ, we must trust him, and not man so that we can survive in these times, so many people are losing their homes, cars, jobs, families all because they put their trust in man, they put their trust in their job, oh if I do a good job my job will be secure, don't you put your trust in man like that, you can be a dedicated worker, and your employer may fire you tomorrow or lay you off for any reason, don't put trust in your family that spouse may leave you tomorrow, your sons, or daughters may put you away in an institution, but if you trust in God, and not in your family, or so many other things in life as Christians if we lose our jobs tomorrow we should trust God that he's got something better for us, if there's no food in the kitchen we should trust him to supply our needs, he cares for the little birds then surely he cares for us, he fed five thousand with two fish, and five loaves after he blessed it, and that's what we should do, trust in God no matter what the circumstance looks like, he's able if you call on him, anything you ask if you ask it in Christ name God said he'd do it, if you abide in him, and he in you, so we just have to exhale, and let God fix it!

Matthew 17:20 says if ye have faith as a grain of mustard seed that we could move mountains, just think how small a mustard seed is, so tiny and if you just have that little smidgen amount of faith then the possibilities are endless to what God can do, don't put a limit on what God can do, there is no limit no matter how things seem, it may look like your bank account is empty, but God said trust him, it may look like you're on your dying bed like I was, but God said trust me, no matter if the physician says, you've got a terminal illness, God said trust me, he's a physician in the bed room, he's an advisor in the courtroom so inhale, and exhale, let go, and let God. You know when a smoker wants that nicotine from a cigarette they inhale, but the smoke can't stay in too long, they have to exhale, and just like when I think about the goodness of Christ, I just start taking it all in my mind, how good the Lord has been to me, but when I think about how much he's blessed me, not once, not just twice, he keeps on blessing me over, and over, and over again, I just have to exhale and let it all out, and say Thank you Lord, Thank you.

When I think about the goodness of Christ, I just get happy. I get so happy I just want to share him with the world. People don't you know how much he loves you, he loves you so much he wants you, and me to live again, he told his disciples in John 14:2 In God's house are many mansions, if it were not so I would have told you, I go to prepare a place for you. In John 14:3 he says and if I go and prepare a place for you, I will come again and receive you unto myself: that where I am, ye may be also. Don't you want to go back with him and live again, I want to go, where there's no more heartache, I want to go where there's no more sickness, I want to go where every day is Sunday, and we can say Howdy, Howdy. Don't you want to go church, don't you want to go my people in this world, won't you come and go with me to God's house, there will be no more wars, and rumors of wars, no more sickness, no more sadness, the streets there are paved with gold, you don't have to worry about losing your house, God in heaven has a mansion just waiting on you it's paid in full, you may say how you know I know cause long time ago on that old rugged cross he paid it all, yes he did, he paid it for you, and he paid it for me, and he has there a mansion for me there too, and what's for you, he's got just for you, and what's for me he's got just for me!

Is there anybody out there who wants to go, if you want to go, will you except him today, he's standing right there with his arms opened wide, that's how he was when he hung his head and deceased, won't you let him in, so you can live again, while the red fluid in your veins is still running warm, Christ is on the main line, just tell him what you want, fall down on your knees and tell him right now, he will answer, he'll answer you today if you are sincere in your heart, call on him today, just call on him, and tell him what you want, he's our God. All you have to do is say Lord I stretch my hands to thee, no other help I know, in hale now exhale he's knocking at your door, now let him come on in for God sent his only, begotten son, that you and I may have a way to the tree of life, now inhale, and let his spirit in, now exhale because you're going to live again.

He's coming back for a church without a spot or wrinkle, Christ will hide a multitude of faults, he doesn't care nothing about your flaws, if you're wrapped up in Christ he'll wash all of your sins away, it doesn't matter what your situation is today, if you're a substance abuser he'll clean you up, if you're an alcoholic he'll dry you up, if you are homeless, and don't have no clothes on your back, he'll give you shelter, he'll dress you up, if you're poor and hungry, he'll fill you up, God is alright, I know he's alright, he's alright with me, and I know he'll be alright with you. In spite of all our difficulties the Word teaches us to consider it pure joy to face trials because you know that the testing of your faith develops perseverance, James 1:4 says perseverance must finish its work so that you may be mature and complete, not lacking anything I understand that had I not went through those things in my life my faith would not have been as strong, I know now without a shadow of a doubt that God was with me thru it all he loves me, and he loves you too, so trust him, trust the Lord in everything that you're going through, Christ has your back, and if you'll just hold on and endure to the end you're going to make it.

And you're going to come out better than you were before, he said in his word in Deuteronomy 28:13 and the Lord shall make thee the head, and not the tail, and thou shall be above only, and thou shall not be beneath. When things get tough God's pulling for you, he's got his angels working in our behalf, so don't be afraid of what the enemy Satan tries to throw at you, if you except Christ then that's all you need he will work it out for your good, as the hymn goes that I used to hear, "Don't Worry Be Happy", and that's exactly what he wants us to do is leave our cares to him, and live the good life that he has provided for us when we obey his word, he has given us basic instructions in the Word, and if we'll obey his word "we will have the good life" that he wants us to have. So inhale and let the good life in, and exhale and let the bad life go so you can breathe again, when you got a friend like Christ who would you be well, you'll find a point when you will exhale. John 1:2 in his word says beloved, I wish above all things that thou may prosper and be in health even as thy soul prosper.

God doesn't want us sick, Satan does, God doesn't want us barely making it on this earth, but Satan does God wants the best life for us while we're here in this life, if sinners can have the good things in life so can people of God. He'll give us the desires of our heart if we abide in his word. Just remember you will have struggles in this life that all goes with being connected with Christ, everyone is not going to like you, you may be ridiculed, scorned, talked about as sure as you're born, there's going to be some suffering, but remember in his word when we do it for his sake, we will live again even if it means dying for some of us don't be afraid for we will gain our life back with him. We must stand up for righteousness, for God's got our back when we endure to the end, for this road is not made for the swift, but to the one who endures to the end. Remember Job, just hold on to our God's unchanging hand, so when you've endured, and you past the test God's got great things in store for you so just take in a deep breath, and hold it in, now slowly exhale, and start waiting to live again! Amen and Amen.

A Families Love

A Families Love is when you need a friend

Someone on whom you can depend

To be there thru thick and thin

Someone to tell your troubles to

Who will always be there for you

Thru the good times and the bad

Even when they make you mad

They cheer you up till you're no longer sad

Someone who always cares

They're like your favorite Teddy Bears

You want to hug them, squeeze them, or greet them with bliss

There's no love like Families Love to be missed

Author: Mildred Watkins

WE ALL HAVE FLAWS IN LIFE NONE OF US ARE PERFECT, SO NO ONE IS ALLOWED TO CHOOSE WHO THEY WANT THEIR FAMILY TO BE, WE ARE GIVEN WHAT GOD GAVE US, AND FOR THAT WE SHOULD BE GRATEFUL. THESE ARE A FEW POTRAITS THAT I WOULD LIKE TO SHARE WITH YOU I AM SO PROUD TO BE A PART OF THIS FAMILY THESE ARE THE PRECIOUS LOVED ONE'S THAT GOD HAS PLACED IN MY LIFE, AND I AM SO THANKFUL THAT HE DID, I COULDN'T HAVE ASKED FOR A MORE LOVING FAMILY THAN THE ONE GOD GAVE ME, AND FOR THAT I AM SO GRATEFUL.

William Jean Valerie

De Lois Anthony

Felicia Sherry

Lenora

Family Portraits

YOU DON'T GET TO CHOOSE YOUR FAMILY THAT'S FOR SURE, AND I WOULDN'T CHANGE MINE FOR NO OTHER IN THIS WORLD, GOD GAVE THEM TO ME, AND I AM GRATEFULL THAT I HAVE THEM IN MY LIFE, ANYONE THAT HAS BEEN BLESSED TO HAVE FAMILY, WHETHER THEY HAVE THE SAME DNA OR ADOPTED IT DOESN'T MATTER WE'RE FAMILY. SO WE LOVE ONE ANOTHER AS GOD LOVES US, MAKE THE BEST OF WHAT YOU HAVE, AND GOD WILL DO THE REST.

Family Portraits

These next few pages are just a few of our family, and friends portrait's that I would like to share with you; I thank God for my family and friends that have been placed in my life.

My Dearly Beloved William We Call June

He loved them Cowboys!

This is my oldest male sibling William, he was named after William Henry Graham Senior you can tell he's a Cowboys fan.

These are all some of my nieces, and nephews at a birthday party
for Ravi On. Top left to right, Tina, Shauntae, Jessica holding
Pinkie, Ravi On, Silas, Navaeh, Miracle, Destiny, and sibling.

Vaughn Felder, friend of the family who has done some acting roles on television, and William Ray Shepherd my nephew in the background

Vision Prosperity Graham at the park

Anthony's spouse Trina at Christmas time

Meme & her spouse Willie

Little Anthony, and sibling Kristle

Ray Ray's daughter Mia, cute as a button

JAZZ, ANTHONY AND TRINA'S DAUGHTER

WAITING TO LIVE AGAIN

A Special
Acknowledgement

TO ALL THE FAMILIES WHO HAVE LOST LOVE
ONES DURING THE COVID 19 PANDEMIC, DURING
THE FINISHING OF MY BOOK. IN THE BOOK OF
REVELATIONS TO THE CHURCH OF PHILADELPHIA
THE WORD SPEAKS OF HOW THERE WOULD BE A TEST
THAT WOULD AFFECT THE WHOLE WORLD THAT
LIVED IN IT, COULD THIS BE THAT TEST THAT IS
GOING ON NOW. THIS IS A TIME WHEN OUR COUNTRY
HAS WENT THRU SOME TRAGGIC MOMENTS, BUT
TOGETHER WE CAN MAKE IT THROUGH IF WE PUT
OUR TRUST IN GOD, FOR HE SAID IN HIS WORD IN 2
CHRONICLES 7:14 IF MY PEOPLE, WHO ARE CALLLED
BY MY NAME, WILL HUMBLE THEMSELVES AND
PRAY AND SEEK MY FACE AND TURN FROM THEIR
WICKED WAYS, THEN I WILL HEAR FROM HEAVEN,

AND I WILL FORGIVE THEIR SIN AND WILL HEAL THEIR LAND.

GOD IS GETTING TIRED OF MAN'S WICKED WAYS, WE AS A PEOPLE NEED TO CRY OUT TO GOD, AND SEEK GOD'S FACE, BEGAN TO LOVE ONE ANOTHER AS WE SHOULD, AS CHRIST SO LOVED US, AND STOP LOOKING AT EACH OTHERS SKIN COLOR AND LOOK AT EACH OTHER AS HUMAN BEINGS JUST LIKE WE ALL ARE EACH AND EVERY ONE OF US, GOD MADE US ALL DIFFERENT, AND UNIQUES IN OUR OWN WAY AS HE CREATED US TO BE, IF HE WANTED US ALL BLACK, WHITE, SPANISH, ASIAN, CHINESE, INDIAN AND SO ON HE WOULD HAVE CREATED US THAT WAY. PEOPLE IT IS TIME TO GET RIGHT WITH GOD, WE MUST GET OUR HOUSE IN ORDER, IT'S TIME OUT FOR NOT GETTING SERIOUS ABOUT OUR RELATIONSHIP WITH GOD IS OVER, GOD IS LOOKING FOR A CHURCH WHEN HE COMES BACK WITHOUT A SPOT OR WRINKLE, IF YOU DON'T KNOW FOR SURE WHERE YOU WILL SPEND ETERNITY YOU NEED TO GET IT RIGHT WITH GOD NOW, TOMMOROW IS NOT PROMISED TO ANY OF US, DON'T WAIT TILL IT'S TOO LATE. FOR CHRIST IS COMING BACK NO MAN KNOWS

THE DAY OR THE HOUR, EACH AND EVERYONE OF US MUST WORK OUT OUR OWN SOUL SALVATION WITH GOD BEFORE IT'S TOO LATE.

WITH THAT BEING SAID THESE TIMES ARE JUST A TASTE OF WHAT IS ABOUT TO HAPPEN IT WILL GET WORSE BEFORE THE END OF TIME, SO STAY IN GOD'S WORD WHILE YOU CAN, IT HAS ALREADY HAPPENED WHERE WE COULDN'T GO TO CHURCH BECAUSE OF THIS PANDEMIC, THAT'S WHY IT'S IMPORTANT TO STUDY HIS WORD NOW, AND GET THE WORD IN OUR MIND'S, AND OUR HEARTS. TIME IS WINDING UP AND IT'S SPREADING RAPIDLY. WE ARE ALL IN THIS TOGETHER, BUT IF SOME OF US DON'T GET IT RIGHT TODAY, IT WILL BE TOO LATE GOD SAID IN HIS WORD, HE WOULD LEAVE ONE AND TAKE THE OTHER, THAT'S ALREADY HAPPENING NOW SO MANY ARE DYING, AND LEAVING THEIR LOVED ONES BEHIND, AND AS THE HYMN SAID OH WHAT A WAY TO LOSE THE ONE YOU LOVE. SO IN MY FINAL WORDS, I PRAY WE'LL ALL BE READY FOR HIS RETURN, CHRIST IS SOON TO COME, NO ONE KNOWS THE DAY OR THE HOUR, BUT GOD IN HEAVEN, SO IT'S TIME TO GET SERIOUS, WE THINK CORONA IS SERIOUS YOU JUST

WAIT TILL THE END OF TIME. PEOPLE "WE MUST BE READY" WHEN CHRIST RETURNS, AMEN! SO LET'S ALL GET IT RIGHT WITH GOD SO WE CAN ALL LIVE AGAIN!

AND THEN SHALL THEY SEE THE SON OF MAN COMING IN A CLOUD WITH POWER AND GREAT GLORY. (LUKE 21:27.)

Final Acknowledgements

Thanks to all my family, friends, and visitors, who were all there for me thru my struggle for without conflict in our lives there would be no strength to make us stronger, and better than we were before so we must persevere because perseverance must finish its course to make us who we can become in this life if you don't give up. Philippian 4:13 says through Christ I can do all things through him that strengthens me. I thank all of you who were there when I needed family and friends the most, your prayers, your time, and the visits will never be forgotten may God continue to be with each and every one of you is my prayer Amen.

Thank you God for your strength to help me endure the pain, the heartache, thru the storm in my journey to making it to this point in my life, thank you so much Lord for sending your precious son Christ that I may have life, and have it more abundantly to the fullest, thanks for all your blessings, and giving me patience, understanding, knowledge, wisdom and showing me so that I can tell the world thru you within me how to live again. I love you Lord forever, and ever Amen.

And finally I want to thank all who have read this book, I pray that it has helped you in some way, and become a divine influence for you to live again, and enjoy this life that God has designed for each and every one of us, be encouraged for the battle is not ours, it's the Lords. Stay in his word for it is the word that will envelop us, keep us, hide us from the enemy and get us thru this life for the word will cover us, until we meet on the other side to another life which is in Gods kingdom in God's word in John 14:2 says I go to prepare a place for you.

Eyes have not seen, nor have ears heard for he has great things for us, so get your house in order and enjoy this life God has given us, and live it to the full, make your life an imprint with the gifts that God has stored inside you so that you too will have made a lasting effect on someone's life before you leave this world, and fly away to a better place called Heaven. I pray to see you there people in Christ name, for all who have, and will accept Christ you too will have that chance in, Waiting to Live Again, Amen!

Printed in the United States
By Bookmasters